Controlling
Your Anger
before It Controls
YOU

Controlling Your Anger *before* It Controls YOU

A Guide for Women

Gregory L. Jantz, PhD
with Ann McMurray

SPIRE

© 2009 by Gregory L. Jantz

Published by Revell
a division of Baker Publishing Group
P.O. Box 6287, Grand Rapids, MI 49516-6287
www.revellbooks.com

Spire edition published 2013

ISBN 978-0-8007-8825-4

Previously published under the title *Every Woman's Guide to Managing Your Anger*

Printed in the United States of America

14   15   16   17   18   19   7   6   5

Contents

5

Contents

Part 3 Uprooting the Anger and Pruning the Branches

Acknowledgments

It seems like every day I have another reason to thank God for the blessing that is my wife, LaFon. I cannot imagine my life without her and I cannot imagine writing this book without her. She is my sounding board, my partner, truly my better half in so many areas of my life. She puts up with me—more, she loves me.

I would also like to thank the many women over the years who have invited me along on their journey to recovery. I may have pointed out an obstacle or two along the way or suggested a different avenue to explore, but the journey has always been theirs. I've been able to witness and experience the miraculous along the way.

Dr. Gregory L. Jantz
Edmonds, Washington

Introduction

Ever felt completely misunderstood? Taken for granted? Stressed out taking care of everyone else while nobody pays attention to your needs?

Ever felt out of sorts, out of shape, and out of options?

Ever felt as though you would just lose it if you were presented with one more thoughtless word, one more careless deed, one more unfeeling demand on your time?

Ever felt really, really angry?

Ever felt guilty about it?

Ever wonder why women get so upset? Why is it that women rage and rant, nag and pester, cry and issue draconian ultimatums? Ever wonder why an argument with a woman and an argument with a man can look totally different, even if the subject matter is the same? Ever wonder, *What is she so mad about?* Ever wonder, *What am I so mad about?*

It is said that hell hath no fury like a woman scorned, but women can be angry about many things besides just failed relationships. Barraged by cultural standards, life demands, physical realities, and spiritual expectations, today's woman feels light-years away from the contented, put-together woman she wants to be. And she's not too happy about it.

Take Janice, for example. She works in a large office as a middle manager. The company recently downsized, and Janice now spends part of her time doing the sort of secretarial work she thought she left behind eight years ago. There's simply more work to do than she can get done in a day, in a week, in a month. The constant pressure is overwhelming. Inside, Janice is seething, especially every time she's given a new project that *must be done immediately*, right on top of the other two she got last week. On the outside, however, Janice never lets on how she feels. She learned growing up that it wasn't polite to show anger. So, at work, Janice is polite. And, in the car on the way home, she carries on imaginary shouting matches with co-workers, her supervisor, and anyone else who got in her way that day. She arrives home feeling exhausted, frustrated, and trapped. Janice doesn't want to take her anger out on her family, but she often does. Now she's feeling guilty on top of being angry. She thinks to herself, *How can I stop being angry all the time?*

(Janice is just the first of many women you'll meet in this book, based on real women I've met and worked with over the years. The names have been changed and the circumstances altered, in order to ensure a level of confidentiality and privacy.)

Or, take Amy. She's a mother of three young children, ranging from four to nine and a half. Divorced for about a year, she's struggling with feelings of rage at her ex-husband, Paul. It feels like he came out ahead on the deal, with the kids on Wednesdays and every other weekend. Amy still has primary responsibility for the kids, both through the parenting plan and because Paul can't seem to be bothered with things like medical visits, running their errands, helping with their homework, or making sure they do their chores. It's playtime when he has the kids, and if there's any sort of conflict with his schedule, he calls and cancels. Paul always has some sort of explanation, but it's impossible for Amy to listen without ending up yelling over the phone. She promised herself she wouldn't get mad at him in front of the kids, but that promise has been broken so many times, she doesn't bother keeping count anymore. Every time the kids either get ready to go to their dad's or come back, her anger spills out on them. Amy knows they're not responsible, but she has so much anger inside it just keeps sloshing over onto them. She thinks to herself, *How can I stop being angry all the time?*

Then there's Marilyn. Her kids are grown, and she's financially secure with established friends and activities. All of the outward pieces of her life appear to be in place; she should be content, but she's not. If she goes out to eat, she complains about the food. If she goes to a store, the service is too slow. It's impossible to watch a movie with Marilyn because of her constant critique. Her friends have stopped sharing any passing annoyances about their day for fear they'll end up being lectured for fifteen minutes on what they did wrong and exactly what they need to do in the future to fix it. With Marilyn, there is no such thing as casual conversation. Nothing is too small to escape the reach of Marilyn's outrage. Her husband now watches the History Channel in the evening so he doesn't have to listen to her running commentary on the nightly news. Either that or he hides away in the den with ESPN. Marilyn sees nothing wrong with her attitude. She's not critical, she's discerning. She's not angry, she's assertive. She's not frustrated, she's problem-solving. She's not negative, she's realistic. She's also not very pleasant to be around. Her family thinks, *How can we get her to stop being so angry all the time?*

How, indeed? Women juggle the bowling balls of family and finances, children and schedules, church and community, work inside and outside the home. Within this time-pressured vise, self-care and personal reflection get squeezed out. Over time, service begins to feel like martyrdom. Over time, each new responsibility, each additional task can feed the flame of anger and resentment.

The injuries and pain of the past weaken the ability to bounce back from frustrating, difficult, or stressful situations. Old wounds, unhealed, break open afresh with present problems. This past-present pain hurts; when you get hurt, you get angry.

Anger can be an empowering, supercharged emotion that shields a person from the inevitable darts of life. But like a drug used to cope in the short-term, anger creates an impossible situation in the long-term. What do you do when your repertoire of responses grows shorter and shorter, with more and more synonyms for rage? What do you do when anger is all you think you have left to feel?

Welcome to *Controlling Your Anger before It Controls You.* This book will take an honest look at anger in general, from a people perspective and from a spiritual perspective. Why just women? Don't men get angry too? Sure, they do. This book, however, will address the situations and pressures that contribute to anger in women. Women have unique reasons for their anger; to counter these, you need to marshal unique resources to overcome anger and live a life of contentment and peace.

People have not generally provided an outstanding example of rational response to anger. Even a brief exploration of history will attest to this unfortunate truth. For many of you, a look at your own past and the role anger has played in your life only provides personal verification that, left to yourself, it's simply difficult to come to grips with your anger. You, like Janice, Amy, and Marilyn, may be tired of asking, *How can I stop being angry all the time?* You've asked that question more times than you care to remember or admit and still haven't come up with the answer. Maybe it's time to look outside of yourself for some of that answer. Through this book, you'll find that a biblically based response to anger has the power to overcome the rage, bitterness, pain, and unhappiness in your life. Using scriptural truths and examples to teach, enlighten, encourage, and motivate, you'll discover:

- the sources of women's anger;
- strategies for living a life free from the anger and pain of past hurts;
- practical steps to evaluate present challenges and difficulties and respond appropriately;
- how to allow God's grace to change past and present anger into appreciation and joy;
- how to create an optimistic, hopeful, and joyful attitude toward life, with whatever it brings.

This book provides answers, offering insight into the emotional, relational, physical, and spiritual reasons for anger in women. More than just providing the "why," this book will provide the answer to "So what do I do about it?"

I realize some of you may be saying, "Excuse me, you're a man! What do you know about a woman's anger?" It's true; I'm not a woman, but I'm married to one and have been for many years. Married for almost a quarter century, LaFon and I are living out God's promise of "one flesh." I have come to understand and appreciate women and what it means to be a woman today in an atmosphere of honesty, transparency, and intimacy. I also grew up around women, especially my mom, Judy. I have a sister and women in my extended family. More importantly, though, I've been in the counseling business for twenty-five years. Over that time, I've worked with many more women than men. Women utilize counseling services to a greater degree than men do, in my experience. Don't get me wrong, I've worked with plenty of men over the years, but often through the efforts of their mothers, sisters, wives, and female friends. The majority of my work colleagues are women.

I've counseled females of all ages, from grade school to the elderly. I've seen their tears, heard their stories, experienced their truths, helped their recovery, and, yes, felt their anger. When their anger is done correctly, it is motivating, empowering, cleansing, and effective. When it's done poorly, it's addictive, self-perpetuating, alienating, unhealthy, and destructive. Many women, however, have never been taught, shown, or modeled how to utilize anger well, if at all. They've been taught to hide it, deny it, defy it—or worse—explode it, feed it, or use it to manipulate those around them.

So, what about you? In this book, I'm not asking you to give up your anger. Anger is an emotion you've been created to experience. What I will ask is that you

- accept the truth of your anger;
- examine where it comes from;
- be honest about how you use it;
- be open to change;
- be willing to forgive, even yourself;
- be willing to let it go;
- be willing to feel something else besides your anger.

My hope is that you're willing, even if it's only willing enough to turn to the next page. There is relief from a life fueled by unrelenting anger and rage, frustration, and irritation. There is a life to be experienced, nourished by a wellspring of optimism, hope, and joy. It's the life you were meant to live. Isn't it time to claim it?

Part 1

The Root of Anger

1

The Role of Anger

When Is It Okay to Be Angry?

Why are you angry? Why is your face downcast?

Genesis 4:6

Anger is clearly a part of life. Most people experience some level of it on a daily basis. Sometimes, anger is appropriate to the circumstances and sometimes it's not. There is a balance to anger that many people haven't learned to negotiate: you get angry about things you shouldn't; you are complacent over things you should be angry about.

The answer isn't to expunge all anger from your life; that isn't possible. Anger is an emotion and a reaction you will continue to feel and experience. The answer is to learn how to craft a role for anger in your life that is within appropriate boundaries.

Because you've found it difficult to come up with those appropriate boundaries for yourself, I offer the boundaries developed by what has been called "a higher power." According to God, there is a list of things that it is appropriate to be angry about. The catch is, the list isn't very long.

The Power of Anger

There are times when it's appropriate to be angry. The issue isn't anger itself, it is the *context* of the anger and how that anger is expressed. God is actually angry a lot in Scripture, especially in the Old Testament. Of course, he has humankind to deal with, so it really doesn't surprise me that much.

God gets angry, and he gave people the ability to get angry too. The role of anger—both God's and humankind's—begins in Genesis and permeates the entire Bible. The words *anger*, *angry*, *wrath*, and *fury* appear around six hundred times throughout Scripture. Reading over all of these references, I was struck by the imagery used for anger and its synonyms. Anger is an extremely powerful and dynamic emotional response. When expressed, it always brings about some sort of change, either to the one who expresses the anger or to whatever or whoever is on the receiving end. Anger is, in other words, highly effective. Listen to how anger and its synonyms are described:

- anger *burns* (Genesis 39:19)
- anger can be *fierce* and *cruel* (Genesis 49:7)
- anger can be *hot* (Exodus 11:8)
- anger *consumes* things like stubble (Exodus 15:7)
- anger can be *aroused* (Exodus 22:24)

- anger can be *hostile* (Leviticus 26:28)
- anger can be *provoked* (Deuteronomy 4:25)
- anger *destroys* (Deuteronomy 7:4)
- anger can be *furious* (Deuteronomy 29:28)
- anger *flares up* (1 Samuel 20:30)
- anger can be *jealous* (1 Kings 14:22)
- anger can burn and *not be quenched* (2 Kings 22:17)
- anger can *break out* (1 Chronicles 15:13)
- anger can be *poured out* (2 Chronicles 34:25)
- anger can come as a *blast* (Job 4:9)
- anger *overturns* (Job 9:5)
- anger can be *unrestrained* (Job 9:13)
- anger *increases* (Job 10:17)
- anger *assails* and *tears* (Job 16:9)
- anger *rebukes* (Psalm 2:5)
- anger *arises* (Psalm 7:6)
- anger *reviles* (Psalm 55:3)
- anger *overtakes* (Psalm 69:24)
- anger *smolders* (Psalm 74:1)
- anger is *powerful* (Psalm 90:11)
- anger is like an *upraised hand* (Isaiah 9:12)
- anger *rages* (Isaiah 30:30)
- anger *surges* (Isaiah 54:8)
- anger can *trample* (Isaiah 63:3)
- anger can be *kindled* like fire (Jeremiah 15:14)
- anger *pursues* (Lamentations 3:43)

Anger, then, is described as a raging fire, with the ability to burn and consume everything in its path. It is portrayed as a destructive change agent. I am, frankly, amazed that God would entrust you and me with so potent an emotion. Yet, he has, so anger has a God-given role to play in your life and mine. The dilemma is to determine what that role is. The challenge is to contain your anger within the boundaries of that God-given role.

God's List

Do you remember when I wrote earlier that there is a list of things it is appropriate to be angry about but that you don't get to dictate the contents of the list? If you asked me today what are ten things I'm angry about, I could rattle them off rapid fire. I know what makes me mad. This list, however, is not necessarily what *should* make me mad. My list would probably tell you more about me and my personality than what truly exists in the world as a source of anger. The ultimate Anger List does not belong to me; it belongs to God. God determines what is acceptable to be angry about. No matter how right, how justified, how clear cut you may feel your anger is, God is the ultimate judge of its appropriateness. No matter how intensely you feel your anger, the depth and intensity of your emotions do not trump God's judgment on the matter.

So, what is God's judgment on anger? What does God deem appropriate to be angry about? Certainly the place to start is back in Scripture, to see what God himself is angry about. God is angry when

- *People oppose God's plans for their lives.* In Exodus 4, God has a job he wants Moses to do, but Moses gives excuse after excuse for why he can't do it. Moses becomes a naysayer to God's plans. This makes God angry at Moses.
- *People use their power to set themselves against God.* Over and over again in the Old Testament, God expresses his

anger at people, including leaders and nations, who go against God.

- *People willfully disobey God's commands.* When people are disobedient and intentionally choose to defy his instructions, this makes God angry.

- *People reject God.* God provided the people of Israel with manna, the bread from heaven, to eat in the wilderness. The people, however, got tired of the manna and began to complain and whine about the "good life" in Egypt under slavery and oppression. They rejected God and his salvation, all because they were bored of eating the same thing every day. They were tired of being God's people and all it meant. They wanted something else; they wanted someone else besides God. This made God angry.

- *People fail to trust God.* After scouting out the land that God promised to give the people of Israel, the twelve spies came back with a report. Ten spies were negative and said the land couldn't be won, even though God said he would do it. Two spies, Joshua and Caleb, were positive and expressed their trust in God to fulfill his promise. The people sided with the ten, making God so angry he refused to allow that generation to enter the land he promised to give them, except for Joshua and Caleb (Numbers 32).

- *People practice idolatry.* When God gave the land to his people, he was quite specific that it was not because of their own righteousness but because of the wickedness and idolatry of the indigenous people. He also warned them repeatedly not to engage in the same evil practices. When they did, he became angry and caused both Israel and Judah to be carried off into captivity (Deut. 32:16).

- *People oppress others.* God has never been happy when people oppress others, in big and small ways—from taking advantage of the powerless, such as widows or orphans

(Exod. 22:22), to cheating people by using dishonest scales (Prov. 11:1). Jesus gives an example of this in Matthew 18, when he tells the story of the unmerciful servant who uses the forgiveness his own master gave to him as an opportunity to oppress his fellow servants.

- *People turn away from God.* One of the saddest stories from the Old Testament is the story of Solomon. I don't mean the first part of Solomon's story, for that is uplifting and amazing. I mean the last part of Solomon's story, where he is corrupted by his foreign wives to sin through idolatry. First Kings 11:9 says that "the LORD became angry with Solomon because his heart had turned away from the LORD, the God of Israel, who had appeared to him twice." When people who have known God specifically turn away from him, that makes God angry.
- *People fail to live up to their word.* God always fulfills his word and every promise made. It angers him, then, when you fail to do the same. This is especially true if you bring God into the promise or the vow. If you swear to do something, you had better make good or God will be angry (Eccles. 5:4–5).

Now, these are some of the things on God's list, but what do they tell you about your own list? Is there a way to look at what God becomes angry about and determine acceptable areas of legitimate anger for yourself? I believe there are some general situations that are cause for what has been called "righteous anger" because they mirror what God is angry about. God becomes angry when his plans are opposed, his will is thwarted, his trust is rejected, his commandments are disobeyed, when those he loves are oppressed. He becomes angry when evil triumphs, good is mocked, sin is chosen, perversion is practiced, vows are broken. He becomes angry when people honor and rely on created things and not the Creator, slipping into useless idolatry.

When Is Anger Appropriate?

God becomes angry when the way things are are not the way they should be, according to his will. Anger, then, is like a warning system that something in the world is wrong. Anger prompts corrective action. There is a major difference, however, that must be factored in when comparing your anger to God's. When God becomes angry because things are not right, he never has to look inward for a reason. When you become angry because things are not right, you must look inward. God is always righteous in his anger; he doesn't need to evaluate it. Because you are not always righteous in your anger, when you become angry, you need to evaluate your reasons, motivations, and actions.

Below are some situations in which I have both seen and experienced anger. I'd like you to take a look at them and place them up to God's template to evaluate whether the anger is justified.

The clerk at the store has to punch in your credit card number because the machine is broken. It's the third time he's put your number in and it's still not right. You're late for an appointment, and a quick stop is going on fifteen minutes and counting. Is it appropriate for you to be angry?

You hear over the radio about a small child who was killed due to abuse by a parent. Is it appropriate for you to be angry?

You've just sat down to read the paper after a long day at work, and your spouse, who's been sitting watching television for about half an hour, asks you to get up and bring back a glass of water. Is it appropriate for you to be angry?

A co-worker knows you're a Christian and makes a point of using obscene language in your presence, repeatedly using the names of God and Christ as swear words. Is it appropriate for you to be angry?

Your teenager tells you he's going over to a friend's house to do homework for the evening. When he fails to answer his cell phone, you call over to the friend's house to find out what time he's coming home. You find out your son has not been there all evening. Is it appropriate for you to be angry?

You're driving down the freeway on your way to work when a car three lanes to your left suddenly diagonals right in front of your car, scooting over to catch a rapidly approaching exit. Is it appropriate for you to be angry?

You're asked to help out at a function at church. You agree to stay late and help clean up. The event is supposed to be over at 9:00 p.m., but it gets started late and doesn't get over until almost 9:40 p.m. You were told there would be at least six people to help with the cleanup, but you find when everyone clears out it's only you and two other people, neither of whom is the person who asked you to help. Instead of taking twenty minutes to clean up, it takes the three of you almost an hour. You're now getting home at almost 11:00 at night and have to get up quite early the next morning. Is it appropriate for you to be angry?

Reading over each scenario, you probably had an immediate reaction, a response to whether or not it was an appropriate situation for anger. Below is my first take on each of these:

- The clerk at the store has to punch in your credit card number because the machine is broken. It's the third time he's put your number in and it's still not right. You're late for an appointment, and a quick stop is going on fifteen minutes and counting. Is it appropriate for you to be angry?

This scenario is frustrating, but there's no reason to be angry at the clerk. It's not the clerk's fault the machine is broken and he's having trouble with the card.

- You hear over the radio about a small child who was killed due to abuse by a parent. Is it appropriate for you to be angry?

As I write this, I hear this story on the news right now. Unfortunately, the names change but the story is horribly familiar. Yes, I'm angry. The fate of this toddler has haunted me all day.

- You've just sat down to read the paper after a long day at work, and your spouse, who's been sitting watching television for about half an hour, asks you to get up and bring back a glass of water. Is it appropriate for you to be angry?

It's certainly annoying when a family member is so engrossed in what he or she is doing that they fail to take you into account, but being angry about this? No. Depending on my mood, I'd either get up and get the water or explain I just sat down and would prefer LaFon get her own water.

- A co-worker knows you're a Christian and makes a point of using obscene language in your presence, repeatedly using the names of God and Christ as swear words. Is it appropriate for you to be angry?

If this were me, I'd be angry about it. I really don't like it when other people deliberately speak in a crude or obscene manner in front of me, especially invoking the name of God or Christ.

- Your teenager tells you he's going over to a friend's house to do homework for the evening. When he fails to answer his cell phone, you call over to the friend's house to find out what time he's coming home. You find out your son has not been there all evening. Is it appropriate for you to be angry?

If this were my son, I'd be angry—angry at being lied to. I'd also be worried because I wouldn't know where he was. Angry and worried—not a very nice combination for a parent.

- You're driving down the freeway on your way to work when a car three lanes to your left suddenly diagonals right in front of your car, scooting over to catch a rapidly approaching exit. Is it appropriate for you to be angry?

I would certainly be irritated if a car suddenly zoomed right in front of me in order to make an exit off the freeway, but I wouldn't be angry, just startled.

- You're asked to help out at a function at church. You agree to stay late and help clean up. The event is supposed to be over at 9:00 p.m., but it gets started late and doesn't get over until almost 9:40 p.m. You were told there would be at least six people to help with the cleanup, but you find when everyone clears out it's only you and two other people, neither of whom is the person who asked you to help. Instead of taking twenty minutes to clean up, it takes the three of you almost an hour. You're now getting home at almost 11:00 at night and have to get up quite early the next morning. Is it appropriate for you to be angry?

This situation probably occurs at churches at least once a month, if not more. It's certainly aggravating if you're on the receiving end of more work than anticipated and less help. I'd want to be angry but hopefully would talk myself out of it. Oh, and I'd sure think twice about saying yes the next time.

Okay, if you tally up my responses, it works out to three "yes" and four "no." What did you come up with? I'd like you to go through the scenarios again, this time delving in a little deeper.

On the Credit Card Fiasco, I said I wouldn't be angry but I would be *frustrated*. How truthful am I being to myself? Can't frustration be another word for anger? Perhaps I used the word *frustration* because I knew it wouldn't look good to say I was actually angry at some poor clerk who was having a bad day. Maybe, though, I actually was angry—angry at being late and trying to do too much in too little time, angry at myself and tempted to take it out on the clerk.

On the death of the child, this one is straightforward; everyone should feel anger and outrage in situations like this. While it's easy to know what to be angry at, it isn't always easy to know who to be angry with. What if the parent is mentally ill and unable to truly comprehend the ramification of the abuse? What if the parent later has a change of heart and expresses remorse? I would absolutely be angry; I would also absolutely want to know *why*.

On the Glass of Water, I said I wouldn't be angry, just annoyed. Again, how honest is that? Isn't *annoyed* another word for *angry*? Maybe I thought I should answer honestly, so I said annoyed, but I really didn't want to say I'd be angry at the sheer cluelessness of a spouse who was so self-absorbed he or she didn't know I'd just sat down! I understand I'm supposed to be a servant to others, but does it really extend to situations like this? What about their unreasonable demands? Isn't it appropriate to rebel against unreasonable demands? Of course, it wasn't really a demand; it was more of a request, and I wasn't obligated to say yes. I could say no. Maybe I'm angry at being put in this situation, where I feel compelled to say yes but really feel like saying no. And feel guilty about it.

On the Cussing Co-worker, I put it's appropriate to be angry. But how is that anger to be demonstrated? If you get angry right back at this insensitive person, is there really an expectation this person will change? Or, will you being angry and upset provide just the reaction this person was looking for in the first place? It's certainly appropriate to be angry at a culture that allows God's name to be trashed verbally, but is an angry response going to change this particular person? The initial reaction is one of anger, but is there a way to use the motivation of the anger to empower you to respond in a different way? Which would be more effective? Anger directed at the co-worker or prayer directed to God about the co-worker? Anger directed at the co-worker or at the condition of the culture?

Okay, what about the Missing Teen? This would make me angry. My teenager looked me straight in the face and lied to me about where he was going to be. I expect to be told the truth, and it really makes me mad when that doesn't happen. Of course, I'm also worried because I realize I have no idea where my child is. Add to that—embarrassment. I'm embarrassed because I called over to the friend's house, only to find out my child wasn't there. Now, that other parent knows my kid lied to me and I don't know where he is. I'm also scared because I have no idea where my teenager is, except it's obviously somewhere he didn't want me to know about in the first place and now he's not answering his cell phone. I'm angry, worried, embarrassed, and scared. All bubbling and popping up to the surface of my mind like some noxious, boiling, emotional brew.

On the Freeway Cutoff, I said I wasn't angry but *irritated* and *startled*. Once I got over being startled, the irritation really began to sink in. What a jerk! That car could have clipped mine and caused an accident! What if I hadn't been paying attention? The more I think about it, the more irritated I become. Of course, irritation is just another word for being angry. I know it's futile to be angry at a stranger I'll never see again, over something that didn't last more than five seconds total, with no real harm done. I know that intellectually, but it's hard not to be mad in the moment and allow that moment to linger far longer than it should.

On the Church Cleanup, these things just happen. Sure, they're aggravating, but churches are essentially volunteer organizations and that's just the way it goes. The person who asked me probably did think they had six people to help out but three of them decided at the last minute not to show or not to stay and help. What's the point in being angry about it? I'll just make sure that the next time that person asks me to help, I say no.

The Next Step to Anger

In each of these scenarios, whether I chose to call it anger or not, I experienced a form of anger. Was it always justified? No. Did I feel it nonetheless? Yes. Is just being angry a sin? I don't believe so. I believe it's what you do with the anger you feel that determines whether or not you sin. There is a progression to how you handle anger that can lead to sin. Look back in Genesis, at what happens when Cain becomes angry.

> Now Abel kept flocks, and Cain worked the soil. In the course of time Cain brought some of the fruits of the soil as an offering to the LORD. But Abel brought fat portions

from some of the firstborn of his flock. The LORD looked with favor on Abel and his offering, but on Cain and his offering he did not look with favor. So Cain was very angry, and his face was downcast.

Then the LORD said to Cain, "Why are you angry? Why is your face downcast? If you do what is right, will you not be accepted? But if you do not do what is right, sin is crouching at your door; it desires to have you, but you must master it."

Now Cain said to his brother Abel, "Let's go out to the field." And while they were in the field, Cain attacked his brother Abel and killed him.

Genesis 4:2–8

That's quite a progression. Cain became angry when Abel's offering was accepted and his was not. But God says that Cain still had the ability at that point to do what was right. Sin was said to be "crouching" at the door; it had not yet entered in. Sin desired Cain in that moment, but God told Cain he could still master it. Cain took his anger, however, and used it to motivate him to murder his brother. If Cain had listened to God, he could have used his anger as motivation to change course and do what was right. Instead, Cain was angry first and then sinned by murdering his brother. It's what you do with the anger you feel that determines whether or not you can be angry and yet not sin.

With God, his anger is straightforward and always righteous. He knows the condition of every heart and the truth of every situation. When he judges, he does so righteously. When he evaluates a situation, his conclusion is always true. You and I, however, don't operate with such a level of certainty. Even in the most straightforward situations of anger, there still may lurk extenuating circumstances, to say nothing of the concepts of forgiveness, mercy, and grace. So, this anger business is a little more complicated than it first appears.

Note to Self

I want you to think about your own relationship to anger. How have you experienced anger in your life? Here are the ways anger was described in Scripture again:

- anger *burns* (Genesis 39:19)
- anger can be *fierce* and *cruel* (Genesis 49:7)
- anger can be *hot* (Exodus 11:8)
- anger *consumes* things like stubble (Exodus 15:7)
- anger can be *aroused* (Exodus 22:24)
- anger can be *hostile* (Leviticus 26:28)
- anger can be *provoked* (Deuteronomy 4:25)
- anger *destroys* (Deuteronomy 7:4)
- anger can be *furious* (Deuteronomy 29:28)
- anger *flares up* (1 Samuel 20:30)
- anger can be *jealous* (1 Kings 14:22)
- anger can burn and *not be quenched* (2 Kings 22:17)
- anger can *break out* (1 Chronicles 15:13)
- anger can be *poured out* (2 Chronicles 34:25)
- anger can come as a *blast* (Job 4:9)
- anger *overturns* (Job 9:5)
- anger can be *unrestrained* (Job 9:3)
- anger *increases* (Job 10:17)
- anger *assails* and *tears* (Job 16:9)
- anger *rebukes* (Psalm 2:5)
- anger *arises* (Psalm 7:6)
- anger *reviles* (Psalm 55:3)

- anger *overtakes* (Psalm 69:24)
- anger *smolders* (Psalm 74:1)
- anger is *powerful* (Psalm 90:11)
- anger is like an *upraised hand* (Isaiah 9:12)
- anger *rages* (Isaiah 30:30)
- anger *surges* (Isaiah 54:8)
- anger can *trample* (Isaiah 63:3)
- anger can be *kindled* like fire (Jeremiah 15:14)
- anger *pursues* (Lamentations 3:43)

Pick out five of these synonyms that describe how you experienced anger growing up.

1.
2.
3.
4.
5.

Looking at your own anger today, pick out five that apply to you right now.

1.
2.
3.
4.
5.

Name five things in the world at large that make you angry.

1.
2.

3.
4.
5.

Name five things about your everyday world that make you mad.

1.
2.
3.
4.
5.

When you are angry, do you feel closer or farther away from God? Why?

God has created you with the ability to experience anger. It is a powerful motivator with the ability to propel action. As with any powerful tool, you need to learn to treat it with respect and use it properly. Only God and his actions and attitudes can provide this example. People tend to mess up anger and end up using it incorrectly and poorly. James puts it this way: "Everyone should be quick to listen, slow to speak and slow to become angry, for man's anger does not bring about the righteous life that God desires" (James 1:19–20). The world will provide all sorts of negative motivations for being angry. When it comes to anger, God must be your guide, not the world. The world's list of what's appropriate to be angry about is voluminous and definitely different from God's in most respects. It's important, then, to recognize where you're being influenced by the world in your anger and how to better be influenced by God.

Father, you are always justified when you are angry. I ask forgiveness for the times I anger you. Help me to discern areas in my life where I am angry but shouldn't be; help me to experience peace. Help me to discern areas in my life where I am not angry but should be; reveal my complacency. I ask you to help me use the anger you have designed within me to accomplish your will and purposes for my life. Prevent me from using anger in ways outside of your will.

2

The Root of
Destructive Anger

*What Part Do Guilt, Shame,
and Fear Play?*

Do not be quickly provoked in your spirit, for anger resides in
the lap of fools.

Ecclesiastes 7:9

If there is an anger that's constructive, there's also an anger that's
destructive. This destructive, hurtful anger is deeply entrenched
in the lives of many. At its root, feeding this anger, are the negative aspects of guilt, shame, and fear. Only by discovering such
poisonous tendrils in your life and behavior can you begin to
uncover it, uproot it, and be rid of it.

Melinda loved a good argument. Of course, to Melinda any argument was a good argument. She could find a way to argue with just about anyone over just about anything. Melinda entered her day poised for battle. As Melinda told her friends on numerous occasions, she was "born ready." No one and no situation was going to get the best of her. She made sure of it.

If Melinda showed red on a color wheel, Darla was a pale blue. Darla never displayed anger of any kind. Instead, she tended to shrug off difficulties and problems, often with a deep sigh, signifying her wish that the world would be somehow different, even while accepting that it never was. Darla shied away from anger, both in herself and others. She made sure of it.

Two different women, two ways of anger. For Melinda, anger is explosive. For Darla, anger is implosive. Melinda displays her anger for all to see, as an early warning system against slights or confrontations of any kind. Darla absorbs her anger deep into her being and camouflages it with a passive, pleasant demeanor. Both women are consumed with anger; they just display it in different ways.

Hidden Anger

The thousand injuries I had borne as best I could, but when he ventured upon insult, I vowed revenge. You, who so well know the nature of my soul, will not suppose, however, that I gave utterance to a threat.

So begins the opening of "The Cask of Amontillado," a short story by Edgar Allan Poe, published in 1846. It is a story of hidden anger, which gives rise to premeditated murder. The main character is a man named Montressor, who puts up with the casual insults and constant slights of a fellow nobleman, named Fortunado, in a nameless Italian village. Over the course of this very short story, Montressor lures Fortunado into a cellar during the revelry of a festival on the promise of tasting a rare vintage wine, Amontillado. There, he calmly chains up his half-drunk nemesis, and brick by brick walls him in the cavern, leaving him to die. Why would Fortunado follow someone of such murderous intent? Because Montressor's anger was a secret so passionate, so private, he kept it hidden from Fortunado's notice.

> It must be understood that neither by word nor deed had I given Fortunado cause to doubt my good will. I continued as was my wont, to smile in his face, and he did not perceive that my smile now was at the thought of his immolation.

Just because anger is hidden does not mean it is harmless. Just because anger is under wraps does not mean it is under control. In the Edgar Allan Poe story, hidden anger leads to death. Over time, Montressor comes to truly hate Fortunado, and this hidden anger and internalized hate provide the motivation for his murderous actions.

Of course, that's just a story. Few people today would confess to harboring this level of animosity toward others. Fewer people today go to such severe lengths as murder. Or do they? God is interested not only in the actions you take but also in the thoughts you harbor. In Scripture, John puts it this way: "Anyone who hates his brother is a murderer, and you know that no murderer has eternal life" (1 John 3:15).

When anger turns to hate, God equates it with murder. What you think matters as much as what you do. It's the same principle articulated by Jesus in Matthew 5:28 when he says,

"But I tell you that anyone who looks at a woman lustfully has already committed adultery with her in his heart." You are responsible for your thought life as well as for your actions. It is vitally important, then, to be aware of hidden anger in your life, even if you've strictly relegated that anger to your thought life.

That was Darla. She never showed any outward signs of anger. Instead, she was always quick to say "yes" even when inside she was screaming "no" or "not again!" Supervisors found Darla compliant but unmotivated. Sure, she got the job done, but it was rarely done completely or in a timely manner. Darla would always agree to come in early or stay late if asked. Because she was so pleasant to be around, they tended to make accommodations and began to think of her as a little slow mentally. So, they tended to give Darla the types of entry level, menial jobs that weren't so time sensitive. Other workers hired after Darla soon surpassed her, moving on to higher levels in the company. Of course, if there was a business downturn, Darla was the first one to go. She'd been let go of a variety of jobs, always reluctantly but with finality.

Darla learned growing up that it wasn't ladylike to display anger. Her father made that very clear, very loudly, very force-fully. She watched as her mother modeled strategies to display her desires or displeasures without ever having to utter a word. One of the ways was to act confused when told to do something she didn't want to do. Darla soon learned her mother really did know what her father wanted done, but the look of perplexity and slow execution were her mother's way of exerting her own control over her life. Darla soon figured out since her father thought her mother was slow, it wasn't much of a stretch for him to assign that moniker to Darla as well.

In her heart, Darla always knew she was better and smarter than her father thought. This knowledge gave her great pleasure, and she would often carry on heated, articulate arguments with her father, all in her head, while completing whatever task he'd assigned, at a deliberately slow pace. He'd always been so surprised at her grades in school, assuming they were a product of the deterioration and "dumbing down" of the public school system.

When Darla entered the work world, she specifically took jobs that were beneath her talents. She chose to keep the true extent of her abilities her own tightly guarded secret. Darla was also fearful of being asked to do a job she truly wasn't capable of, that was above and beyond her abilities. It was important to her that her father's low opinion of her never be confirmed. So she worked at her own pace, for her own reasons, internally mocking her supervisors and secretly feeling superior for their failure to recognize her true potential. Darla didn't think of herself as angry; she thought of herself as clever, hiding behind her smile. She didn't see the problems this behavior brought, only the protections.

Burying anger does not diffuse it; rather, it tunnels it underground, where it undermines your sense of self and manifests in damaging ways. Sometimes, the need to deny the strength of, or even the existence of, anger is so powerful that you create the capacity to deny the anger even exists. But the force of the anger will find other, secondary outlets. Dr. Roland Mairuo, MD, of Harborview Medical Center in Seattle says, after twenty plus years in anger management, "Anger is such a powerful coping mechanism that repression and suppression are not successful. The more you try to avoid it, the more time and energy you are going to spend with it. It's a paradox."[1]

Even if you hide your anger, you are still spending time and energy on it. Following are some ways I've observed hidden anger manifested.

Procrastination in the completion of tasks, especially ones you don't like or want to do. There are myriad ways to exert control over your environment, based on how you feel. Even if you do not show outward anger, you can still communicate those hidden feelings through ancillary actions, such as not completing tasks you don't want to do on time or failing to complete them altogether. You show your true feelings about something through your actions, if not always your words.

Habitual lateness. By your actions you demonstrate how you really feel. James makes this point in his book, in regards to faith, making the connection that you can know whether or not a person has faith by what he or she does. I would argue that the same applies to anger. Whether or not a person *says* they are angry, I can generally tell whether or not they are angry by how they act. Now, granted, some people are late because they are very unorganized and have trouble getting anywhere on time. I have heard this rationale from many I've worked with on this issue. However, the same people seem able to arrive on time to those events they genuinely wish to be at. For those events, they make the effort. For the rest, their lateness makes the point.

Sarcasm, cynicism, or flippancy. Often, these strategies are done as a joke or portrayed in a lighthearted manner by the quick-witted and verbally adept. They are also done by those deeply wounded and angry but who are afraid to confront directly. These strategies provide the cover of "plausible deniability." If ever confronted about the remark being hostile, the person can plead a misunderstanding in an attempt to maintain the hidden nature of the anger behind their remarks. The focus is then moved away from the speaker of the remark and is concentrated on the perception of the listener, in order to divert attention away from the true feelings behind the sarcasm, cynicism, or flippancy. The joke exists as protective covering for the anger bubbling under the surface.

Overpoliteness, constant cheerfulness (fake), attitude of "grin and bear it" but internally resenting it. This is classic passive-aggressive behavior. My late friend Cynthia Rowland-McClure had one of the best analogies for passive-aggressive behavior I've ever heard. She said it was like a dog that licked your face while it peed on your leg. Taken to its extreme, as in "The Cask of Amontillado," a passive-aggressive Montressor is smiling and pleasant with Fortunado, all the while planning to kill him. In its more mundane forms, passive-aggressiveness is a pattern for all kinds of discontent against people and situations in life. The goal is to hide the anger, not eliminate it. In fact, some people can actually have a secret anger-life where they spend a great deal of time and energy internally resenting their life, situations, and people.

Frequent sighing. Sighing can be an outward, physical sign of inner turmoil. Not only is it a physical release, it is also an audible sign to those around you. If you sigh enough around others, someone will eventually ask you, "What's wrong?" The answer to which, for those who hide their anger, is "nothing," but the sighing doesn't stop. It is a physical signal of discontent, even while the person who uses it denies its presence.

Smiling while hurting. This is not referring to those brave individuals who are able to find the silver lining in the darkest cloud. These are the people who are caught in the storm and refuse to acknowledge the deluge. These are the people who attempt to minimize and marginalize their pain. This is dishonest and does not help a person face the reality of their situation. For honesty in the midst of struggles and overwhelming odds, I can think of no better place to go than the psalms of David. Over and over again, David is quite descriptive of the problems he faces. He does not attempt to sugarcoat them. Listen to some verses out of Psalm 69 as an example:

> Save me, O God, for the waters have come up to my neck.

> verse 1

> I am worn out calling for help; my throat is parched. My eyes fail, looking for my God.

> verse 3

> I am in pain and distress; may your salvation, O God, protect me.

> verse 29

> I will praise God's name in song and glorify him with thanksgiving.

> verse 30

I do not envision David smiling through this time of trouble in his life. This does not mean that David was somehow unfaithful in his understanding of God. On the contrary, David, through his distress, always acknowledges God's love and faithfulness, as in verse 30. God does not expect you to deny the pain you feel, as some sort of act of righteousness. Denying the pain you feel and putting forth a false front comes under the category of self-righteousness.

Overcontrolled monotone speaking voice. It is good and right to control your tongue. First Peter 3:10 says, "Whoever would love life and see good days must keep his tongue from evil and his lips from deceitful speech." You can easily understand the "tongue from evil" part, but I submit that an overcontrolled monotone speaking voice is "deceitful speech." It does not convey the reality behind your words. Keeping your voice so tightly controlled may seem like a way to avoid angry words, but it does nothing to resolve what caused the anger in the first place. Instead, it drives the anger underground, where it continues to fester.

Frequent disturbing or frightening dreams. When anger is driven deeply into your subconscious, it finds fertile ground for expression. Whether or not you choose to acknowledge the anger, it will surface. Often, it finds a conduit in the realm of sleep. You may deny that you're angry when awake, but the content of your dreams will often reveal the truth.

Difficulty in getting to sleep or staying asleep. Thoughts going around in your head keep you awake. Unresolved anger is a constant irritant. It seeps into your thought life and can dominate it. The longer the anger remains hidden and unresolved, the louder it becomes until it screams in your mind when the world gets quiet. There is no rest, no sleep, no relief from anger's internal clamor.

Boredom, apathy, loss of interest in things you are usually enthusiastic about (depression from internalized anger). When the accumulated anger reaches a boiling point, it can either explode outward or implode inward. When it implodes inward, it leads to depression. When the pain is too great and seems impossible to deal with or work through, many people decide the only way to cope is not to feel anything at all. Apathy appears to be preferable to anger, but the apathy only attempts to smother the anger. In doing so, it also smothers happiness, joy, and pleasure, leading to depression. The anger isn't gone; now, it fuels the depression.

Slowing down of movements, especially when doing things you don't want to do. This is akin to procrastination and often is the next step. Once the unwanted activity is undertaken, you can still communicate your dislike and disapproval—your anger at having to do the activity in the first place—by deliberately retarding your own progress. It is a form of self-sabotage, hampering your own actions as an act of defiance.

Getting tired more easily than usual. Anger is a volatile, active emotion. It is energetic. Because of this, even the act of hiding it takes energy and effort. The more energy and effort funneled into this hidden anger, the less there is available for simply living out your life.

Excessive irritability over trifles. Internalizing anger and keeping it there builds up tremendous pressure inside. Often, this pressure finds release by small bursts of anger at commonplace, ordinary things. A person who would never dream of speaking up for herself to a supervisor may become enraged at a perceived slight by a co-worker. A person who shrugs off the stress of an ever-increasing load at work yells at her child over a forgotten homework assignment. A tightly controlled professional reverts to profanity over being cut off while driving. The little things in life become the release valve for a deep wellspring of anger. This produces what I've come to think of as a "high IQ—Irritability Quotient." High IQ people are like volcanoes just waiting to vent through the side pockets and fissures of everyday occurrences.

Facial tics, spasmodic foot movements, habitual fist clenching, and similar repeated physical acts done unintentionally. Again, anger is energetic. Even when buried, it has a way of finding physical release.

For many women, especially those raised in an earlier generation, anger was considered inappropriate. The expression of anger was frowned upon and considered validation of the "unstable" emotions of women. Therefore, anger in women was ridiculed and dismissed. Angry men were decisive and forceful. Angry women were shrewish and shrill. Women expressing anger were considered disrespectful.

There was a nursery rhyme I remember growing up. It went something like this:

> What are little boys made of?
> Snips and snails, and puppy-dogs' tails.
> That's what little boys are made of.

It had a companion:

> What are little girls made of?
> Sugar and spice, and everything nice.
> That's what little girls are made of.

Boys were allowed to grub around with snails and play with dogs and get dirty and roughhouse and, yes, express anger. Little girls were to be all sugar and spice and everything nice. Anger wasn't considered nice. Little girls, if they did get angry, were not to show it, but instead were to hide it, to pretend it didn't exist. So, the anger got stuffed down, hidden. Little girls like Darla were taught to avoid feelings of anger, irritation, annoyance and, if felt, to avoid expressing them at all costs.

One of the ways I see hidden anger manifested in my line of work is through eating disorders. Many eating disorders, especially anorexia, are rage internalized to self-hatred and fury. There are few things besides this level of anger and rage capable of fueling the iron-willed commitment to self-starvation.

Vented Anger

Melinda didn't get that anger message growing up. Or, if she did, she soundly rejected it. Melinda gave free vent to her anger at all times, in all situations. Anger was her expression of choice. Of course, if you asked Melinda, she was never responsible for her anger. Other people and situations *made* her angry. She went through life constantly being provoked by the carelessness, stupidity, mistakes, selfishness, shortsightedness, rudeness, and outright attacks of others. Therefore, her anger was explainable and justified. She was not responsible for her anger; she was merely responsive with her anger. At least, that's what she told herself.

When Melinda was angry, she felt powerful and invincible; she felt vindicated and not at fault. This was very important to her as an adult because of what happened to her as a child. When Melinda was a child, she felt powerless, damaged, responsible, and guilty. Melinda had been sexually molested by her grandfather from the time she was five until she was twelve and the family moved away to another city.

An attractive child, Melinda was the first daughter sandwiched between two brothers. Both of her parents worked in the family business started and run by her grandfather. No one in the family—from her grandmother to her mother to her father to her uncles—ever said no to her grandfather. His word was law and his temper legendary. The path of her molestation ebbed and flowed during the years, depending on his health and her availability. Melinda always suspected her parents, especially her mother, were aware of what was happening, but she was too frightened to say anything at first and too ashamed later. There were parts of it she came to like—the attention, the "little princess" status she held in the family, the candy and gifts she received.

The older she got, however, the more physical the abuse became. She began to view herself as a sacrificial offering of the family to her grandfather, in order to keep him happy and keep the peace. But Melinda became angrier and angrier the older she got and was punished for her disrespect. When she was twelve, with pubic hairs emerging and her period not far away, her grandfather stopped all of his attention to her. His health turned precarious, as did the health of the family business. The family decided to move away to start over in a different town. Her grandfather was furious, blaming her parents for running out on his life's work. Upon his death a few years later, they received nothing and were bitter and vocal about it.

It seemed to Melinda her sacrifice had been in vain. She'd ultimately been rejected by her grandfather, as had the rest of the family. Every "positive" she'd consoled herself with during the abuse turned out to be for naught. With him dead, there was no way to confront her grandfather as she became older. No confrontation, no closure.

Melinda, however, found plenty of outlets for her rage. She determined she would never put herself into such a vulnerable position again. She hated her parents for their docile reliance on someone she came to view as a monster. Determined not to repeat that pattern, she went to school to establish her own professional career, dependent on no one but herself. Melinda became an architect. She was soothed by the finite nature of architecture and the way all the pieces were supposed to fit together. That never seemed to happen when she was a child, and she relished the order and symmetry.

Distrustful of relationships and scarred from intimacy, Melinda kept people at bay with her anger and forceful personality. In school, her anger fueled her superior grades. In her career, her anger stoked the flames of professional competency and a relentless desire to be better than all expectations. In relationships, her anger protected her from any possibility of being taken advantage of again. It also alienated anyone she might have wanted, in a weak moment, to get close to.

True to Scripture, Melinda's anger was a raging fire. The older she got, the less able she was to keep it under control. The older she got, the more she began to realize her anger was less of a protective positive in her life and more of a destructive negative. The only problem was she felt naked, exposed, and vulnerable without it—just like she'd felt with her grandfather.

Guilt and Shame

When you feel hurt, it is normal to feel anger. Anger is a cue to respond to a harmful situation. Anger is a motivator to act when you feel threatened. That is what anger is designed to do and, as such, is a positive. But anger becomes complicated when it is provoked by the negative aspects of guilt, shame, and fear. The intensity of anger, hitched to the pervasive power of guilt, shame, and fear, can become an overwhelming force in your life, whether that anger is vented to all around you or stuffed down deep inside yourself.

There are few things as devastating to self-esteem and sense of self as the shame that comes from feeling guilty. This guilt eats away at your sense of self; it's always in the background, poisoning every good thing and every good thought. Guilt is the knowledge you are less than you should be. Shame is an inner acknowledgment that the worst that could be thought of you is true. Guilt and shame remove your ability to stand up for yourself because you don't feel worthy to stand. Even as I write this, it makes me angry to think of the women I've known who live a life seeped in guilt and shame for events and situations over which they had no control. Assigning guilt and shame is a common tactic of an abuser, whether the abuse is sexual, physical, or emotional. Guilt batters you with, "It is your fault!" Shame screams, "You are to blame!" Guilt and shame remove all escape from the pain; instead, they force you to bear the pain full force, unprotected.

Please don't misunderstand me; there are times when you are guilty. When your actions are wrong and you realize it, you should be ashamed. The Old Testament prophet Jeremiah says, "After I strayed, I repented; after I came to understand, I beat my breast. I was ashamed and humiliated because I bore the disgrace of my youth" (Jer. 31:19). The proper time for feeling guilty is after you stray—or after you do something wrong. Shame is a powerful motivator to repent, change your ways, and do the right thing the next time.

But what happens when guilt is assigned to you and shame comes through no fault of your own? What happens when guilt and shame are thrust upon you by the actions of others? What happens when you are weighted down with the guilt and shame someone else refuses to rightly carry? When you feel guilty and ashamed, it's easy to be angry at yourself for your vulnerability, stupidity, carelessness, worthlessness. Guilt knows all of the negative vocabulary of self-recrimination. Shame says you deserve whatever you got, and more. Shame becomes your accuser.

Children are often saddled with the guilt and shame of others' actions. Because children are vulnerable and naïve, they believe what they are told. They have a natural tendency to view themselves at the center of events and therefore as responsible, whether or not they are. Children of divorce, for example, often internalize the failure of their parents' marriage as their own fault.

In a way, I've always found this a remarkably courageous thing to do. By internalizing responsibility, the child attempts to maintain some sort of control over an uncontrollable situation, believing, "If I'm only good enough, my parents won't fight" or "If I do well enough in school, my daddy won't move away." When children have been saddled with the guilt and shame of others, they accept responsibility for the pain inflicted on them. By accepting responsibility, they attempt to exert control.

Melinda, as a child, came to accept responsibility for her abuse. Because she felt responsible for the horror happening to her, she was angry at herself for the pain she felt. As she aged and began to look at her abuser with older, wiser eyes, she began to understand the double injury done to her—the actual abuse and the shame it caused. Her earlier anger at herself was diverted into fury at her accuser. There was only one problem; he was dead. When she confronted her parents, both of them swore they had no idea and gave her the impression they suspected she had imagined or embellished the whole thing. Regardless, they made it clear they didn't want to talk about it. Her brothers were sympathetic but didn't remember any such behavior directed at them, so it was easier to dismiss her accusations than to deal with the fallout. Their only recollection of their grandfather was that Melinda was clearly his favorite. With her family's reactions, Melinda decided it was up to her to protect herself in any and all situations, and she vowed she would always, *always*, be up to the task.

Fear

Have you ever had someone play a practical joke on you by hiding around a corner, then jumping out with a loud shout?

What is your first reaction? If you're like me, you get a jolt of fear. You're startled and caught off guard. This usually is followed up by the person laughing over your unguarded reaction and shocked expression. It is also usually followed by your flash of anger at the person for scaring you like that. Being afraid can make you angry. The more fearful you are, the greater the anger you feel.

Do you remember the scenario in the first chapter about the teenage son who wouldn't answer his cell phone and wasn't even at his friend's house? I said I'd be angry, embarrassed, and scared. Fear usually opens the door, and anger walks right in.

No one likes to be truly afraid. I recognize there are plenty of people who enjoy watching a scary show or engaging in the free fall of a thrill ride, but this is fear contained, fear managed, fear controlled. It is all the thrill of fear within the comforts of security. You know the movie will end and the ride will be over. You're able to laugh and enjoy it because you know there's an end. Anger comes when the movie keeps playing and the ride doesn't stop.

For some people, this is the content of their lives. For some people, even though the movie is over, they're still stuck in the theater; even though the ride is over, they still feel as if they're suspended in air, feet dangling, waiting for the bottom to drop out. Fear is a constant companion. Even when events are peaceful, they live in fear that something will change. When their lives are burdened down with problems, they're fearful one more struggle will undo them completely. They're fearful of what happened yesterday, what will happen today, and what may come tomorrow. As a consequence, they are anxious about their situation and angry at having to live this way.

Because their anger comes from a base of fear, it is often desperate, unreasonable anger. It is the husband who refuses to allow his wife to work because he's afraid she'll find someone else and have the means to leave him. It is the mother who refuses to let her son develop his own life for fear he'll grow up and leave her alone. It is the wife who refuses to engage in consistent intimacy with her husband for fear he'll find her physically unattractive. It is the father who refuses to let his daughter wear makeup or date for fear she'll become promiscuous. When inner fears are pricked, the response can be desperate, unreasonable fear expressed in anger and rage.

Note to Self

I'd like you to take some time and examine how the anger you feel is vented out to the world around you and how it is funneled inward. There are some of you who will completely recognize yourself in Darla and others who, if honest, must call yourself a Melinda. However, the majority of you are a little bit of both. Whichever you are, in whatever percentage, it is important for you to begin to identify the avenues your personal anger takes.

Because hidden anger is camouflaged, I'd like you to look over again the signs of hidden anger and put a check mark by any that relate to you. Really look each of them over and take a moment to think about your life, your interactions with other people, and how you operate on a day-to-day basis. It's fine for you to sit a while and think about each one. This isn't some sort of timed test. The more honesty and thought you put into it, the greater insight you'll gain about yourself. Trust me, it's worth it. (Oh, and expect to be surprised. Hidden anger isn't called hidden for nothing.) After each box you check, indicate whether this behavior is constant, frequent, or occasional.

☐ Procrastination in the completion of tasks, especially ones you don't like or want to do

☐ Habitual lateness

☐ Sarcasm, cynicism, or flippancy

☐ Overpoliteness, constant cheerfulness (fake), attitude of "grin and bear it" but internally resenting it

☐ Frequent sighing

☐ Smiling while hurting

☐ Overcontrolled monotone speaking voice

☐ Frequent disturbing or frightening dreams

☐ Difficulty in getting to sleep or staying asleep. Thoughts going around in your head keep you awake

☐ Boredom, apathy, loss of interest in things you are usually enthusiastic about (depression from internalized anger)

☐ Slowing down of movements, especially when doing things you don't want to do

☐ Getting tired more easily than usual

☐ Excessive irritability over trifles

☐ Facial tics, spasmodic foot movements, habitual fist clenching, and similar repeated physical acts done unintentionally or unaware

Look over and identify those behaviors that are constant or frequent. For each one you marked, ask yourself the following questions.

1. Why do you believe you have this behavior? State a reason that explains this pattern.

2. Are you able to identify a source of anger, irritation, or frustration at work within that behavior?
3. How long has this behavior been true for you?
4. Do you remember when you first noticed it?
5. Do you remember any significant events in your life happening around the same time?
6. Has anyone around you commented on the behavior? If so, what was your response?
7. Have you ever wished you could stop this behavior?
8. Have you ever tried to stop? If so, what was the outcome?

For those you marked occasional, ask yourself the following questions.

1. When did you first notice this behavior?
2. Looking back over the past six months, has this behavior increased, decreased, or held steady?
3. Have you ever been able to link a past event or feeling with this behavior in the present? Do you have any idea where it's coming from?
4. Has anyone around you commented on the behavior? If so, what was your response?

Over the next several weeks, I'd like you to keep coming back to this list and keep these behaviors in the forefront of your mind. Be aware when you engage in them and, if you're able, write down how you're feeling at the moment you realize you're doing them. Keep track and see if any patterns emerge that might help you identify a source for the behavior. Anger, especially hidden anger, needs to be peeled back in layers, to get at the heart of the issue. Give yourself the time you need and the permission to explore this area of your life.

Vented anger, because of its "out there" nature, can be much easier to identify. However, many people still attempt to diffuse it by calling it other names, as you saw briefly in the earlier chapter. I'd like you to take a look at the following list of words and mark any you identify as part of your anger repertoire. Again, be honest and bold. If you have a loved one or close friend, consider asking him or her to look over the list and discuss it with you. Other people are a good barometer of what you aren't able to recognize in yourself.

- ☐ disappointed
- ☐ bitter
- ☐ resentful
- ☐ critical
- ☐ controlling
- ☐ hostile
- ☐ mean
- ☐ sarcastic
- ☐ frustrated
- ☐ insecure
- ☐ victimized
- ☐ destructive
- ☐ anxious
- ☐ irritable
- ☐ impatient
- ☐ blaming
- ☐ manipulative
- ☐ selfish
- ☐ prideful

All of these can be ways of expressing anger. Look over your list and answer the following questions.

1. What do you tell yourself when you feel this way?
2. Does your thought life escalate or deescalate your feelings?
3. How do you feel after you express these feelings?
4. How do you feel about yourself?
5. How do you feel about anyone else involved?
6. How do you feel physically?
7. How long does it take you to get over the feelings?
8. Do you "replay" the event and the feelings inside your head?
9. Are you ashamed of how you reacted?
10. Are you remorseful over how you reacted?
11. If you could get rid of one of these reactions, which one would it be and why?

Be aware of your anger levels over the next several weeks. Again, write down, if you're able, what you feel and any reasons you determine for feeling that way. Note any out-of-line or extreme reactions or feelings. Be sure to write these down for more examination, thought, and prayer.

Anger can happen so easily, so smoothly attuned to the autopilot of your daily life. For the next several weeks, I'd really like you to live your life in "manual," with a hands-on, alert spirit. This isn't meant to make you more distressed but rather to help you identify the things you need to work on and avenues for prayer.

Above all, remember you have an active partner in this process. Just as God said to Cain, he says to you: "Why are you angry? Why is your face downcast?" (Gen. 4:6). There is a why to all this, a why that can be determined and brought out into the light.

Father God, thank you for loving me enough to engage me in this conversation over my anger. I give this process and, ultimately, my anger over to you. Help me be diligent in seeking answers and not revert back to old habits that are harmful to me, to others, and to our relationship. I rely on your grace through this process and ask that your Holy Spirit speak to me and reveal truth. Help me not be afraid but to trust you as I learn and grow in this area.

Part 2

The Branches of Anger

= 3 =

How Do Unfulfilled Expectations Affect Anger?

Esau held a grudge against Jacob because of the blessing his father had given him. He said to himself, "The days of mourning for my father are near; then I will kill my brother Jacob."

Genesis 27:41

One reason you get angry is because life hasn't turned out like you expected—unfulfilled expectations. Perhaps for you there was supposed to be a knight in shining armor, meaningful and rewarding work, an attentive spouse, a white picket fence, happy and obedient children. Adulthood was supposed to mean you were finally in control. Instead, it appears you've been sold a huge bill of goods that's anything but good. If you're angry about it, get in line. The line for "it wasn't supposed to turn out like this" is a long one. Just get in line, right behind Esau.

Esau was supposed to have the preeminent position in his family. As the firstborn, he was to receive the birthright, which was established in Deuteronomy 21:15–17. The birthright was a double portion of inheritance. But instead, the birthright went to his twin brother, Jacob, who was born second. Esau, as the firstborn, expected to receive his father's primary blessing prior to his death. Instead, Jacob received the first blessing. Things didn't turn out as Esau had expected, and he became angry, bitter, and bent on murder.

In the anger and bitterness over unfulfilled expectations, most women don't resort to murdering others; most will merely kill off their own ability to be happy.

Colleen was never happy. Instead, she contended every day with a life battered by unfulfilled expectations. By her age, she felt she was supposed to be more successful than she was, more attractive than she was, more loved than she was, more obeyed than she was, more in control than she was. No matter how hard she tried, no matter how much she wanted, bad things kept happening to her. It seemed as if all the things she kept grasping for kept slipping out of her hands. Sometimes, they were simply yanked out of her hands, and she was furious about it.

Colleen never saw herself divorced at forty-three. She was supposed to still be married, but Tim had made that impossible.

She was supposed to be financially independent and able to have a little breathing room. That was impossible now on a single income. She felt like she was back twenty years ago, having to decide between gas in the car or a new pair of shoes.

At least she still had the house, but it needed painting, which Colleen couldn't afford. Neither of the kids were thrilled about doing yard work, so weeds grew and bushes overgrew and the house took on a semi-abandoned look, which caused glares from the neighbors, none of whom offered to help.

By now, Colleen was supposed to have figured out a way to lose those extra thirty-five pounds. Of course, with her life in such a shambles, that was impossible. The thirty-five was now closer to fifty.

She was supposed to have obedient, well-mannered children. Instead Colleen had a mouthy, angry daughter who blamed her for the divorce, and a withdrawn, sullen son who rarely gave her the time of day. They were supposed to be allies in the breakup of the family, victims together, and instead they treated Colleen like the enemy.

She wasn't supposed to be working so hard with so little recognition. After all the time, energy, and effort she gave to her job, Colleen was supposed to be rewarded and recognized. Instead, they kept complaining because of all the time off she requested, even when she was sick.

Colleen was angry because life, her life, seemed totally out of her control, as if there was some sort of malevolent puppet master manipulating the strings of her life to send her falling on her face and crashing into obstacles. It was so unfair and so different from what she thought her life was going to be like. Each disappointment kept adding to the anger, piling on top of the problem the hour before, the irritation the day before, the frustration the week before. Colleen kept wondering when she was going to get a break before she had a breakdown. In the meantime, she seethed.

Colleen tended to blame others for her present difficult situation in life. This isn't particularly novel; people have been doing this throughout time. In Scripture, Esau also felt himself a victim of others, specifically to the deceptions of his brother,

Jacob. When Esau realized Jacob had received the blessing from his father meant for him, he cried out, "He has deceived me these two times: He took my birthright and now he's taken my blessing!" (Gen. 27:36). That statement is not the truth. Jacob did not take Esau's birthright; Esau sold it to Jacob for a bowl of stew (25:29–34). Esau wasn't deceived about the birthright; he knew what he was doing (v. 33). But in the intervening years, Esau's version of events and his own culpability were colored by his anger at Jacob. Over time, Esau despaired and raged because he thought himself an innocent victim of Jacob's deception. In reality, the only deception about the birthright was his own refusal to view it honestly. Esau wasn't powerless, but in order to deny his own culpability in the way his life turned out, he chose to view himself as powerless, as a victim, and this added to his rage.

The Power of Truth

Colleen felt powerless to control a life spinning out of balance. So many women I work with have this perception of their lives. They feel they are puppets on a string, directed how to act, what to say, when to move. It is as if they are adrift on a raging river in a small boat without any oars, at the mercy of the wind and the current, terrified of what lurks around the next bend, with no way to control the boat. In short, they feel victimized by life and their circumstances. Because they feel powerless, they are unable to recognize the truth of the power they really do have over their own lives.

Esau had the power over his birthright. He was the first-born, so no one could take his birthright away from him; it was codified in Scripture. Esau had the power and he gave it away, on a whim. He bartered away his future to satisfy the desires of the present. He was not deceived, as he later claimed, for Jacob would not allow Esau to sell the birthright until he made an oath, a formal declaration, before receiving the food. There was no "I was just kidding" aspect to this. Esau knew what he was doing at the time. After Esau gave the oath and sold his birthright, Genesis 25:34 says, "Then Jacob gave Esau some bread and some lentil stew. He ate and drank, and then got up and left. So Esau despised his birthright." All along, Esau had the power to keep possession of his birthright; he could have simply refused Jacob's trade and made his own lunch. Esau chose not to do that. And instead of accepting the consequences of his own actions, he blamed Jacob.

Similarly, Colleen felt powerless because she refused to see the part she played in the circumstances of her life.

She wanted to blame Tim for the breakup of their marriage, even though her attitudes and actions were also responsible.

She wanted to blame Tim for her loss of income, when it was the court who decided his obligation was to provide financially for the kids but not for her.

She felt victimized because, even though she got the house, with the house came household, yard, and neighborhood responsibilities, for which she was ultimately accountable. Instead of accepting these responsibilities along with the asset, Colleen chose to be angry about it, blaming her kids and her neighbors.

Her weight gain was a direct result of daily decisions she made, but Colleen blamed everything and everyone but herself.

Colleen blamed her children for adding stress to her life while denying the fact they were both hurting and wounded themselves and in no position to minister to her.

It was easy to blame her employers for being insensitive, even though the chaos in Colleen's life negatively impacted her ability to do her job.

Colleen chose to use her anger as a screen to avoid seeing her own responsibilities. Blinded to her own responsibilities, Colleen was unable to comprehend and appreciate her own power. Unable to recognize her own power, Colleen felt powerless. Feeling powerless increased her anger. And so it went, the cycle turning in on itself, spiraling Colleen's life and anger out of control.

It is so easy to be like Esau and Colleen. People have well-developed denial systems and ways to shift blame away from self, even in the best of times. There are enough realistic expectations that go unfulfilled in this life that it is not helpful or healthy to fixate on unrealistic expectations that quite naturally go unfulfilled. Realistic expectations flow from the truth of actions and situations. Unrealistic expectations, by their very nature, will generally go unfulfilled.

- How can you expect to be still married if you have contributed to the marriage's demise?
- How can you expect to be taken care of financially by someone else when you have separated yourself from that person?
- How can you expect other people to undertake responsibilities that rightly belong to you?
- How can you expect to lose weight when you consistently refuse to make healthy choices?
- How can you expect hurting children to respond like adults?
- How can you expect an employer to constantly overlook a poor job performance?

These are not realistic expectations; they are wishful thinking.

Wishful Thinking in Unfulfilled Expectations

A wish is a very powerful thought with an emotional context. Merriam-Webster's online dictionary gives this definition of wishful thinking: "the attribution of reality to what one wishes to be true or the tenuous justification of what one wants to believe." The overriding factor in a wish is not what *is* true but what you *want* to be true. If your sense of fairness and satisfaction in life is based on a wish and not on reality, life will always be unfair and unsatisfying.

Esau wanted to believe he had the favored status because he was the favored son. After all, his father Isaac clearly loved him best (Gen. 25:28). Esau thought this favor would translate into supremacy in the family. This was not the truth, however, for God ordained something different. In Genesis 25:23, God spoke to Esau and Jacob's mother, Rebekah, and said of the twin boys prior to their birth: "Two nations are in your womb, and two peoples from within you will be separated; one people will be stronger than the other, and the older will serve the younger." God turned the status upside down, making Jacob higher in status than Esau. Was this fair? Was this right? Regardless of how you feel about it, it was the truth.

Colleen wanted to believe that others should be responsible for her circumstances. She wanted her ex-husband to bear the responsibility of the marriage dissolving. She wanted to have more money without earning it herself. She wanted other people to step forward and relieve her of the normal responsibilities of being a homeowner. She wanted to lose weight without having to make changes. She wanted her children to rally to her aid instead of exhibiting their own brokenness. She wanted her job to just look the other way until she got her life back together, however long it took.

Those wants weren't based on the truth, so as long as she pinned her happiness on things that weren't true, she was bound to be disappointed. Disappointment, day after day, led to a wellspring of anger. Overwhelmed with anger, bitterness, and frustration, Colleen had no room to experience anything else—certainly nothing positive—for very long.

Without even really being aware of them, Colleen was influenced by key assumptions she held about herself, about life, which led to her wishful thinking and unrealistic expectations. These were deeply rooted in her sense of self and perceptions of the world. Colleen believed:

- *I need to be perfect to be happy.* Colleen believed an ordered world would be a happy world, so she set out to control as many people and events as she could. This stranglehold of control was one reason her marriage failed.
- *When I am upset, it is the responsibility of others to comfort me.* Growing up, Colleen came to rely on the intervention of others to handle her own discomfort, whether it was her parents who gave her things to placate her and make her happy as a child, to friends and lovers who were expected to mitigate her discomforts as she grew older. This even included her children, who were expected to put their own needs on hold whenever Colleen was upset.
- *When others harm me, it is intentional.* When injured, Colleen learned to lash out in anger. It was difficult for her to believe in and allow for the mistakes of others, especially when she held herself to such a rigid standard of perfection. If others hurt her, it was because they meant to do it.

Colleen did not allow others the escape clause of a mistake she granted herself.

- *When I harm others, it is a mistake.* Because of her need to see herself as perfect for her sense of self-worth, Colleen was loathe to admit she did anything worthy of forgiveness. In order to maintain her high opinion of herself, Colleen needed to believe that the harm she brought to others was insulated from any actual intent on her part. As a mistake, the harm was separate from herself and became the responsibility of circumstances beyond her control.

- *The more intense my pain or discomfort, the less the rules apply to me.* As the weight and burden of perfectionism increased as she was growing up, the more the ideal became impossible to maintain. When the floodgates of her frustration burst forth, so did her anger. It was in times of such emotional surge that Colleen felt free of the chains of perfectionism. The rules she set for herself no longer applied because of the intensity of her feelings. When she got "this way," she was no longer responsible. The responsibility was shifted to those who caused her to get "this way" in the first place.

- *I deserve to be taken care of by others.* Growing up, Colleen assumed this was the contract she had with her parents. If she was perfect, by their definition, then they were obliged to provide for her. After all, if she got As in school, she received rewards. If she looked attractive, she got clothes. If she followed all their rules, she got a car. Because she came to see herself as perfect in so many aspects of her life, she felt she should be catered to by others as a reward for her stringent efforts in this regard. She was *due.*

- *Others must carry my burdens for me.* Part of being taken care of, in Colleen's mind, was being relieved of burdens.

When she was a child, her parents never required her to work or pay for what she wanted, as long as she was "perfect." It was a shock, therefore, when she moved out of the house and realized how hard it was to care for herself. It wasn't long before she met Tim and they got married. She assumed Tim understood his part of the contract, the quid pro quo. Because Colleen was operating within her idea of perfection, Tim was thus obligated to relieve her of whatever burden she demanded.

- *If I am angry, no one else has the right to be.* This was an axiom she learned from both her mother and her father. No room was big enough for both of their tempers, and certainly she was no match for either of them. As she got older, she learned to route her anger into different avenues, so she could still enjoy her anger but suffer none of the consequences of revealing it. Once she left her parents' home, she could give free rein to her considerable anger. She got to be the "parent," and everyone else was expected to follow her childhood example of concealing any anger they might have.

Colleen based her life on false assumptions that she developed when she was growing up. The more time and energy she put into the wishful thinking of these false assumptions, the less able she was to see and operate within the truth. Wishful thinking springs from pain, disillusionment, misunderstanding, and longings from the past. As such, they are amazingly powerful illusions. I have known women who have lived with them clouding their lives for decades.

It takes courage, perseverance, and faith to come to an understanding of the falsehoods in your life so you can begin to counter them with the truth. The only thing powerful enough to do this, I firmly believe, is God's Spirit. God's Spirit is called "the Spirit of truth" (John 14:16). In order to overcome the false assumptions underlying her wishful thinking and unrealistic expectations, Colleen needed a dose of the truth from God's Spirit, revealed in God's Word.

- Happiness comes from an inner contentment, not a manipulation of outside circumstances. *(Phil. 4:11–13: "For I have learned to be content whatever the circumstances. I know what it is to be in need, and I know what it is to have plenty. I have learned the secret of being content in any and every situation, whether well fed or hungry, whether living in plenty or in want. I can do everything through him who gives me strength.")*

- When you are upset, you are able to find comfort within yourself. *(Ps. 119:49–50: "Remember your word to your servant, for you have given me hope. My comfort in my suffering is this: Your promise preserves my life.")*

- When you are harmed by others, the actions can be either intentional or accidental and more often than not require grace. *(Col. 3:13: "Bear with each other and forgive whatever grievances you have toward one another. Forgive as the Lord forgave you.")*

- It is possible to harm other people even when you don't want to and perhaps more importantly when you do want to. *(Rom. 3:23: "For all have sinned and fall short of the glory of God.")*

- The standards of conduct in life and relationships apply to all circumstances, including times of distress and discomfort. You don't get to determine your own areas of "exception." When Colossians says "whatever" and "all," those include everything, including difficult, trying, and challenging circumstances and situations. *(Col. 3:17: "And whatever you do, whether in word or deed, do it all in the name of the Lord Jesus, giving thanks to God the Father through him.")*

- Your greatest fulfillment will come when you serve others, as exemplified by Christ. *(Mark 10:45: "For even the Son of Man did not come to be served, but to serve, and to give his life as a ransom for many.")*

- As you learn to shoulder your own load, you gain strength to help shoulder the load of others. *(Phil. 2:4: "Each of you should look not only to your own interests, but also to the interests of others.")* Load carrying is reciprocal, not one way. *(Gal. 6:2: "Carry each other's burdens, and in this way you fulfill the law of Christ.")*

- People often react to the anger of others by being angry themselves. This only results in nonproductive arguments. *(2 Tim. 2:23: "Don't have anything to do with foolish and stupid arguments, because you know they produce quarrels.")*

The only way for Colleen to get control over her life was to realize she had that control all along. Instead, she decided not to see the control she had because of the way it was tied up with responsibility. Instead, like Esau, she'd bartered away something precious for something cheap; she'd exchanged the truth of her own responsibility for an illusion of others being responsible. Because she didn't want the responsibility, she abdicated the control. By accepting the responsibility, she rediscovered the control.

A Season for Truth

Self-delusion is amazingly powerful. There are some people who are able to uncover their own delusions and denials by themselves, in the normal course of time. Often, however, uncovering delusions and denials are brought about by tragic or traumatic events. People are, in essence, shocked into truth through a death, a divorce, a job loss, an illness, a family crisis, or when a long-held secret is revealed. These things can shatter the veneer of delusion into a shower of razor-sharp revelations. Already reeling from the initial blow, people may find it extremely difficult to assimilate the truth and overcome the desire to remain desperately in denial. Frankly, this is often when women wind up seeking professional help.

I'm not saying that it isn't possible to deal with your delusions and denials in the midst of crisis. It happens all the time. But what I often hear women lament is a desire to have known and understood the truth sooner. Once the false assumptions behind all that anger and frustration, agitation and ferocity are revealed, a realization of how much precious time, love, happiness, understanding, reconciliation, and peace have been lost takes place. They wish things had been different. They wish they had dealt with their own issues earlier, because it was hard to deal with those on top of everything else going on.

I hope you're not in the midst of a crisis, but I'm realistic enough to realize many of you are. Keep reading and working. It is possible to get through the storm of circumstance on the outside while navigating personal turmoil on the inside. The time is now to deal with your anger issues. This is your Season for Truth. It may not be what you consider an ideal time, but whenever you recognize your anger as an issue, it's the right time to deal with it.

Ecclesiastes 3:1–8 says:

> There is a time for everything,
> and a time for every activity under heaven:
> a time to be born and a time to die,

a time to plant and a time to uproot,
a time to kill and a time to heal,
a time to tear down and a time to build,
a time to weep and a time to laugh,
a time to mourn and a time to dance,
a time to scatter stones and a time to gather them,
a time to embrace and a time to refrain,
a time to search and a time to give up,
a time to keep and a time to throw away,
a time to tear and a time to mend,
a time to be silent and a time to speak,
a time to love and a time to hate,
a time for war and a time for peace.

I especially like verse 6 when it comes to dealing with the false assumptions behind unrealistic expectations. It says, "A time to search and a time to give up, a time to keep and a time to throw away." Unrealistic expectations are your desires searching for a reason to be validated; if they are not based in truth, it is time to give them up. There was a time when it was very important for you to keep and hold on to those false assumptions, probably while you were growing up. Now you're an adult and it's time to throw them away. They've produced more than enough anger, envy, jealousy, bitterness, and hate up to this point in your life—so much so that love has been crowded out. You've been at war with yourself and others for so long—isn't it time for peace?

Note to Self

False assumptions are the foundation for unrealistic expectations. Unrealistic expectations produce a crop of bitterness, anger, and rage. It's time to uncover the truth, confront the false-hood, and reduce the fuel for your anger. Truth can be extremely cleansing; it can also be extremely painful.

Pain, however, does not automatically negate the benefit of the truth. Paul, writing to the Corinthians, talks about this dilemma of truth causing pain. In an earlier letter, Paul wrote the truth about their behavior to the Corinthians, and this was hurtful to them. He says: "I see that my letter hurt you, but only for a little while—yet now I am happy, not because you were made sorry, but because your sorrow led you to repentance. For you became sorrowful as God intended and so were not harmed in any way by us" (2 Cor. 7:8–9). Dealing with the truth, although painful, can be used by God for his purposes, for repentance and reconciliation.

Truth in your life defuses rage and moves anger into appropriate channels. First, however, you need to discover what the truth is. Searching for truth is like digging for treasure; usually you have to make your way through a lot of dirt. This "dirt" is the false assumptions that get layered over the truth through time. Colleen had developed quite a thick layer of false assumptions over the course of her life. As a recap, here they are again:

- I need to be perfect to be happy.
- When I am upset, it is the responsibility of others to comfort me.
- When others harm me, it is intentional.
- When I harm others, it is a mistake.
- The more intense my pain or discomfort, the less the rules apply to me.
- I deserve to be taken care of by others.
- Others must carry my burdens for me.
- If I am angry, no one else has the right to be.

Here are some other false assumptions uncovered by women in their personal work.

- No one works harder than I do.
- The people in my life now must make up for the pain caused by the people in my past.
- I am always taken advantage of by others.
- I am supposed to deny my own needs for the needs of others.
- Men cannot understand what it means to be a woman.
- Women are more understanding and intuitive than men.
- Women are better than men.

I'd like you to take some time uncovering your unrealistic expectations and the false assumptions underlying them. This can be difficult to do because of the power they have in your life and thoughts. Start first with these false assumptions from Colleen and the additional ones I've provided. These are by no means meant to be an exhaustive list. Rather, I'd like you to read them over and put a star next to those that resonate with you. Note I said *resonate*; it doesn't have to be one you're completely ready to sign off on right now. Instead, if something inside of you twinges just a bit as you read it, or causes you a second glance, go ahead and star it. Read over them now.

Go back to the list and read aloud every one you've starred. Put yourself firmly in the "I" position. Examine your thoughts and your feelings. Ask yourself, "How true is this for me?" Underline each statement you feel is true for you.

There is a reason why you underlined each of the statements chosen above. You want each statement to be true. This may seem harsh or contradictory, but you do not hold on to false assumptions unless you want them to be true. Otherwise, you would convince yourself they weren't true and would operate under either another false assumption or find your way to the truth. Instead, these false assumptions are the ones you have chosen to keep. It is important for you to admit you want them to be true. Please write them down below.

What I Want to Be True

1.
2.
3.
4.
5.

(I put down room for five. Some of you will have fewer and some will have more. If you have more, please write down any additional ones on a separate piece of paper, or write all of them down together on a separate piece of paper. Also, please recognize that you are not "better" if you have fewer or "worse" if you have more. This is about being honest and coming face-to-face with your false assumptions. This is good work you are doing. It's not some sort of graded test. Just be honest and let the numbers fall where they may—or, rather, where God intends, as Paul says in 2 Corinthians.)

Remember, these were provided to give you a starting point. Each of you will probably come up with one or even several false assumptions, playing off these provided, that are unique to you. Again, each person is different, with their own personal circumstances. If the false assumptions that hold power over your life aren't listed, then write them down as you meditate on these and look to overlay them onto your own life and thoughts.

Next, I'd like you to answer why you'd like each false assumption to be true. For an example, Colleen wanted the following statement to be true: *I need to be perfect to be happy.* Here is how she would have answered this next part about why:

> I want this statement to be true because then I am in control of my own happiness. My own efforts, not the effects of others or circumstances, will control my happiness. I do not want anyone else to have that much power over my own happiness. I've tried that before and it hasn't worked. If I control my own happiness, I can insulate myself from the pain of life and of others. I am afraid of what will happen when I am not in control.

For each statement you've underlined, please search your heart and your thoughts, your hopes and your fears, and write down the why. In my line of work, there is always a why, even when the person I'm working with vehemently denies it or professes not to know it. The why, again, is almost always layered over and difficult to uncover.

This exercise may not be one you can do all in one sitting. If not, that's fine. Take one statement at a time and work through it, following the trail of the truth to its core. Again, this is important work and well worth the time and effort.

Some of you will be able to immediately come up with a reason. You'll triumphantly write it down and stamp it as the truth. Just a word of caution: in my experience, it's not quite as quick and "easy" as that. You're going to need to spend some time with this. Read over the statements again and again. Look at them, examine them, examine yourself. Read over what you've written and "live" in that statement for a while. Look at it from different angles.

Most of all, pray about it. The Spirit of Truth lives inside you, and according to John 16:13, one of his functions is to "guide you into all truth." This is something you can revise and revisit as you grow and the truth is revealed to you. Write down thoughts that startle you or ones you aren't sure about but want to explore further. There is no right or wrong answer here. There is no extra credit for doing this all in one sitting. Do your best now but recognize this is an exercise you can keep coming back to over the entire course of the book.

Next, I'd like you to write down what *is* the truth. You have identified what you need to be true and why, as much as you're able right now, for each statement. Now, I'd like you to identify, as close as you can, what the actual truth is. In the example I gave from Colleen, her actual truth is summed up in the last sentence: *I am afraid of what will happen when I am not in control.* As much as you are able, cull down your statements into identified truths about yourself and what really lies at the heart of your anger. A main source of Colleen's anger was fear.

Written exercises are great; however, I believe there is value in expressing ideas and concepts artistically. Over the years, I have seen women produce works of astonishing clarity and insight that only came about because it tapped into a different part of their brain.

For this exercise, I'd like you to get a blank sheet of paper and an assortment of crayons or markers. If you don't happen to have any in the house, make an initial sketch with pencil or pen. However, please go out and either buy or borrow crayons or markers. It is important to express yourself not only through drawing but also through color. Your brain is an amazing instrument and you cannot know just what it will take to unlock the door to layered truth. Please do not dismiss or put off this exercise!

Take your piece of paper and fold it in half. On one side, whichever side you'd like—either right or left—I'd like you to draw a picture of your false assumptions. What are they to you? Are they a shield? A wall? A mountain you can stand on where no one can reach you? Are they a weapon you hold with arm outstretched, protecting yourself from the world? Are they a cave where you feel safe and protected? How do you see them in your mind? I want you to draw them with all the positives you believe them to have.

Next, I'd like you to draw what they really are on the other side of the paper. They're not a shield of iron; they're a shield of straw, which allow the illusion of protection while leaving you unprepared. They're not a wall keeping pain out; they're a prison keeping pain in. They're not a mountain perching you above problems; they're a pit with no way out. The weapon isn't pointed outward; it's pointed inward. The cave isn't safe and protected; it's filled with all sorts of anger, malice, and rage.

This is the sort of artistic work often done in chemical dependency and other groups at The Center, assisting people to identify the truth of their addictions. (The Center is a whole-person healthcare facility treating mind, body, and spirit with mental health, medical, nutritional, and chemical dependency services.) In a way, you are addicted to your own false assumptions and unrealistic expectations. You feel you need them in order to survive and are reluctant to give them up. Only by naming them for what they are and standing firm in the truth can you begin to work your way beyond them.

Some of you will be able to work through these exercises by yourself. Others may seek out a trusted friend or loved one to process these questions with. Some of you may simply find yourself at a loss, not really knowing how to navigate through your false assumptions and unrealistic expectations. Please do not construe this as some sort of failure on your part. Instead, view it as a signal you need to enlist the aid of someone trained to deal with these sorts of issues. I encourage you to seek out the help of a professional counselor. If you were having trouble with your finances, you'd go to an accountant. If you weren't feeling well, you'd go to a doctor. If a tooth was bothering you, you'd go to a dentist. Going to a counselor or therapist is really no different. You are seeking out those people trained to assist you in addressing your issues. Shame over asking for help comes from the negativity of false assumptions. Don't listen! If you need assistance, seek it out, grab hold of it, and use it.

Throughout the next several weeks, as you continue to refine your understanding of the false assumptions and unrealistic expectations you hold that fuel your anger, be prepared. Anytime you undertake work to uncover and live in the truth, you will face spiritual opposition. Deception, lies, falsity, and delusions are favorite chains used by Satan to bind people to their anger. In this battle to become free, you need to unleash the power of the Spirit and prayer. As you feel comfortable, ask for the prayers of those who love you and of your faith community. Anger is a common struggle, and I believe you will find more compassion and understanding than condemnation if you confess your need.

Some people are uncomfortable praying. If you are one of these people, I suggest you find a prayer partner. This is a person who will commit to praying for you, with you, and also separately.

If you find yourself having difficulty knowing what to pray for, write down what you need and pray through what you've written. In my books, I have endeavored to end each chapter with a prayer. I encourage you to use this prayer daily or as often as you need it. Write it down on a small card; memorize it if it is difficult for you to know what to pray for yourself. Use it as an example and personalize it.

Most of all, open yourself and your heart to God. Discover where it is easiest for you to talk to God. For some people, it is on their knees. For others, it is walking outdoors with plenty of space to wrestle with their thoughts and with God. For some, prayer is silent; for others, it's loud. Find your own prayer patterns and use them. This is challenging and important work you're doing, and prayer is an integral part of the work.

Holy Father, I know there is no shadow of falsehood in you. You are truth itself and want me to live in truth. I ask you to hold my hand as I walk through discovering the truth in my own life and thoughts. I confess I have wanted my false assumptions more than I wanted the truth. Give me courage and peace to accept the truth because sometimes the truth really hurts. Be with me when I hurt because of the truth. Heal me when I hurt because of the truth. Strengthen me with the understanding that truth is important to you so it needs to be important to me. Remind me of the truth of your love, grace, and forgiveness as the underlying truth of all else. Teach me your truth, Father. Set me free.

=== 4 ===

What's Wrong with Keeping Score?

But if you harbor bitter envy and selfish ambition in your hearts,
do not boast about it or deny the truth.

James 3:14

Most women act as the family "historian," with an uncanny ability to recall details and events in complete clarity and focus. Women are record keepers. This is a wonderful quality and one I've relied on over the years. If I fail to recollect an event or remember a name or recall an important point, I go to my wife, LaFon. If it's something from my youth, it's as close as a call to my mother, Judy. For both of them, whatever I can't remember is usually on the tip of their tongue, and the memory comes rushing out as clear and crisp as an autumn day.

This amazing ability, however, has a dark side for women. Women can take it and use it to remember every injury or insult, every unkind word or misunderstood event, every vacant stare or broken promise—in short, every wrong ever perpetrated against her. As James 3:14 says, this type of negativity often finds safe "harbor" in your heart. But, what if a misspoken word is just that? What if an unfulfilled promise was a simple mistake? What if event Z has no valid connection to event A? A single act today, woven together with all the rest, can create a tattered cloth of anger, outrage, and indignation.

Ethan and Emily cast a quick glance at each other, simultaneously communicating both dread and hope. Rachel, their mother, had narrowed her eyes and taken a deep breath, and both of the kids knew they were about to get it, double-barreled. The only bright spot was they were in public so it wouldn't be as bad as at home.

"Why do you kids keep asking me for things you know you can't have? You drive me crazy with your constant whining!" she hissed loudly, visibly frustrated and upset. With increasing strides, Rachel took off down the grocery store aisle without looking back, assuming the kids would follow in her wake.

"You shouldn't have asked for those markers," Emily said quietly, walking along slowly.

"You said you wanted them too!" Ethan objected, feeling hurt she was making it all his fault. He didn't know why he'd asked. He'd known what would happen, but these were the markers with thirty-six different colors instead of the eight his set had. These were the thin markers that looked more grown-up than the fat kind he'd gotten at the start of school. He'd been afraid to say anything bad about those when his mother bought them because they'd been on sale and he was happy just to have something. But he'd already been kidded about his "baby markers" by a few classmates. Besides, he really wanted more colors to use with his drawings. It made him feel bad to have to keep borrowing from the other kids.

Ethan and Emily followed behind Rachel, with a shared understanding there would be no more "requests" during this shopping trip. If they were lucky, she would be over her anger by the time they got home. Until then, they walked carefully, on guard and watchful of her temper.

Up ahead, Rachel fumed. It was hard enough putting food on the table without these constant demands for more things from the kids. They had no idea what it was like to have to stretch a dollar and keep track of every purchase. What did Ethan need with that many markers anyway? The ones she's gotten at the start of school were just fine. It was always "more" with them. More stuff, more clothes, more games, more toys—just more. It was like that all her life. Everyone she was around always seemed to want more from her. Why couldn't they see how hard it was for her? Why did they keep wanting more when she was trying as hard as she could just to get by?

As Rachel steered her cart down the aisle, she was furious, picking out items from her list on autopilot, engaging in a silent battle in her head, railing against the pressure put on her by others. It never seemed to change, never seemed to get any better. She was starting to believe she had some sort of target on her back, or a big sign that said "Kick Me." Why else would people always want more than she was able to give? Why else was her best never good enough? It was bad enough when it was her parents when she was a kid, and her siblings now, always wanting things from her. Couldn't they see how hard she was working?

Why couldn't they give a little bit to her for a change? But, no. It was even that way at work. No matter how hard she worked, it was never good enough.

Turn by turn, Rachel wove her way through the grocery store. Turn by turn, she wove the threads of her anger tighter and tighter together until her heart raced and her head felt like it would explode.

As she neared the checkout line, she looked back to see where the kids were. They were there, trailing behind as usual. Part of her was glad the kids seemed to read her mood and give her lots of space; she felt bad about yelling at them. Part of her wished they would ask for something else, so she could relieve some of the pressure building up. It wasn't fair she had to hold it in all to herself.

Record Keeping

The fabric of your life is made up of all the threads you choose to hold on to. Every event, every circumstance, every impression produces a thread. It is important, therefore, to be intentional about the threads you choose to keep.

There is an interesting verse in Scripture that talks about these threads. Oh, not in that way, of course, but the concept is similar. The book of Luke starts out with the story of the birth of Christ. In the second chapter, the Bible speaks of how the shepherds in their fields at night saw the glory of God proclaiming the birth. Excited, the shepherds go into town and find Mary, Joseph, and the baby Jesus, and tell of all the amazing things they've seen and heard. Verse 19 says, "But Mary treasured all of these things and pondered them in her heart." I've always liked that verse because it provides a little bit of insight into the remarkable woman who was the mother of Jesus. Mary took in what was happening around her, what was being said about her child and about herself. She treasured these things and tucked them deep into her heart. Mary kept a record; she wove a thread. These amazing events would help sustain her in the confusion and heartache to come. Perhaps she even thought of the things of his birth at his death.

Women remember a great deal. They also can have difficulty letting hurtful things go. Again, Scripture speaks about this propensity to hold on to things. In the apostle Paul's first letter to the Corinthians, he gives a beautiful treatise on love in the thirteenth chapter. I would venture to say this passage is one of the most beloved and quoted in all of Scripture.

> Love is patient, love is kind. It does not envy, it does not boast, it is not proud. It is not rude, it is not self-seeking, it is not easily angered, it keeps no record of wrongs. Love does not delight in evil but rejoices with the truth. It always protects, always trusts, always hopes, always perseveres.
>
> 1 Corinthians 13:4–7

That's a very tall order. I want you to especially think about the part that says "it is not easily angered, it keeps no record of wrongs." When you keep a record of wrongs, when you choose to weave in threads of hurt, resentment, pain, frustration, irritation, and negativity into the fabric of your life and thought life, you will become easily angered. Or, put another way: if you keep a record of wrongs, you will be easily angered. When you are easily angered, the table is set for the poison of resentment to take up residence in your heart. Paul cautions that, in order to love, you have to keep the right kind of records; you need to weave in the right kind of threads. Keep the wrong kind and you will be an angry person.

I can't remember all the studies I've seen over the years, but it has become almost conventional wisdom that to counter a single negative, you have to have multiple positives. Maybe you've heard something similar, that it takes ten positive statements to counterbalance a negative one. I don't know about the actual numbers, but negatives just seem to carry more weight than positives do. I've seen it in others and felt it in my own life.

I have spent a good deal of my professional life speaking at seminars and giving interviews. Of course, I always want to do a good job whenever I speak. Invariably, after the seminar is finished or the interview is over, I'll go over in my mind how it went. If I'm not careful, I'll end up dwelling not on what I did say but on what I should have said. And if, heaven forbid, I should mix something up or say it differently than I meant to, I have a tendency to fixate on that. One misspoken word can threaten my view of the entire event.

It's not just me; it is human nature and the power that negatives have in life. It's why it takes so many positives to counteract the negative. It's as if you don't quite trust the veracity of all those positives, while the one negative becomes proof positive. If just one negative, one "wrong" has such weight, can you imagine the critical mass generated by an extensive "record of wrongs"? This pressure becomes overwhelming, producing anger, frustration, irritation, and often rage.

If you look at the example given of Rachel, the mother of Ethan and Emily, she definitely kept a record of wrongs. Ethan's request for markers at the store touched a sore spot. Rachel didn't have the money to get her groceries and buy her son the bigger, more expensive set of markers. She reacted to his request in anger because she felt he was asking for something she could not give. This touched a nerve because it was a feeling Rachel had felt over and over again during the course of her life. When she was confronted with a question that made her feel that way again, the anger that overwhelmed her had little to do with the question itself. The question was merely a trigger, the crack in the dyke that allowed the floodwaters of frustration and anger to burst through. Ethan's innocent question was interpreted as a "wrong" and was added by Rachel to the storehouse of wrongs she maintained inside her heart.

This reaction, or overreaction, is often referred to as pushing someone's buttons. Just a simple tap on this button from even a casual remark or unrelated event releases a backlog of resentment and rage, frustration and irritation. This is the bitter pool that negativity draws from. The deeper the pool, the greater the flood when released. The greater the flood, the more positives it takes to dam up and contain the bitter waters again. Ethan's question punched Rachel's button. The result was not good for anyone.

Chewing the Cud

When you keep a record of wrongs, you house this stockpile of negatives inside of you. Because they are events, circumstances, impressions, and feelings of the past, they require you to bring them up and keep them fresh in the present. If you didn't keep them fresh and present, they would eventually fade from view, shoved aside by other things. In order for all these negatives to stay in the present, they require you to *ruminate* on them.

Ruminate means to "go over in the mind repeatedly." To ruminate is to think about something over and over again. It comes from the same root word that refers to animals chewing the cud. I'm not an expert on cows by any means, but I've heard they have multiple stomachs. In order to digest grasses and grains, they perpetually chew a little, swallow, and then bring it back up and chew it again. This is a secondary definition of ruminate: "to chew again what has been chewed slightly and swallowed." That is hardly an appealing picture, but it's what you do when you draw from your bitter pool of negativity. When you ruminate in your mind on all your record of wrongs, you're acting like a cow chewing the cud. But, instead of chewing the cud, you're really chewing the *crud*. You're re-chewing all that negative crud represented by your record of wrongs. When you ruminate, you recycle your pain. It's no wonder engaging in this kind of mental activity produces bitterness, anger, resentment, and rage.

Neutralizing Negativity

The goal of love, according to the apostle Paul, is to keep no record of wrongs. This is no easy task. With so much negativity in the world and with the added power of the negative to influence thoughts and feelings, you may be wondering how to counterbalance such a force. Paul says it's necessary to experience and embody love. I believe women have a deep desire to love, to love well, and to love better. This desire to love better is a powerful motivation to find a way to neutralize the negativity. Through intentionality and staying alert to yourself, you can develop strategies to neutralize negativity in your life and begin to reduce your backlog record of wrongs. I have found the following to be effective:

- Pick out the negative threads.
- Pounce on the positive threads.
- Treat yourself gently.

Picking Out the Negative Threads

Have you ever watched someone knit? I remember being mesmerized by a friend who was knitting something—the hypnotic motion of the knitting needles and her hands as she wove the yarn into a colorful pattern. Imagine my surprise when she stopped after a while and began to yank on the end of the yarn, unraveling a good portion of her work! Astonished, I asked her what in the world she was doing. She explained that she'd made a mistake earlier in the work, something about dropping a stitch. In order to give the piece the integrity it needed, she had to go back to that point and take out the flawed section. She had to remove the negative thread.

This is a metaphor for what you need to do in your own life to remove negativity. You need to "unravel" the threads, going back to the parts causing negativity, so they can be pulled out and redone. This is the work of therapy. This is the work of recovery and restoration. This is also the work of a wonderful lady named Cynthia Rowland-McClure, whom I mentioned in an earlier chapter.

Over the course of her life, Cynthia had built up a huge storehouse of negativity, secreting away in her heart a record of wrongs, from insensitive comments by others to childhood insecurities, from unrealistic expectations about the future to painful injuries in the past and present. A bitter pool of anger built up inside Cynthia, supplying the rage needed for her eating disorder. Because of the poison inside, no amount of positives in Cynthia's life could counteract even the smallest perceived negative. All of the successes she experienced were suspect and every failure validation of the extent of her negatives. As she would come to realize during her journey to recovery, Cynthia believed herself to be "damaged goods." She felt inferior and unworthy. In her pursuit to gain her understanding of perfection so she could finally feel good enough to be loved, appreciated, and validated, Cynthia gave in to the false promises of bulimia. She found herself binging for hours a day and horribly abusing laxatives.

Bent on ending her life and relieving herself of the pain she felt, Cynthia cried out to God to rescue her because she knew she couldn't do it on her own. Praise God because he did, leading Cynthia to undertake a road to recovery and wholeness that led her to write an amazing book about her struggle with bulimia called *The Monster Within*. Through intensive therapy, Cynthia had to unravel her past and pull out the negative threads woven into her perception of herself and her life. Then, she began the task of lovingly reworking her life. She undertook Ephesians 4:31 in the real world, removing those words from some sort of abstract ideal and actively, purposefully, intentionally doing what those words say: "Get rid of all bitterness, rage and anger, brawling and slander, along with every form of malice."

Cynthia came to realize she felt that negativity, not about other people primarily, but about herself. She was bitter about her life and the negatives she saw there. She was full of rage at the damage done to her. Through her eating disorder, she turned her anger inward and used it to fuel her bulimia. Inside, she brawled with herself over her own self-worth and value.

Through her low opinion of herself, she slandered herself in her mind every day. Through her eating disorder, she treated herself with malice, causing pain and distress.

Cynthia needed to unravel those negative threads and rework love back into her life. She had to start by learning how to love herself. Because of a traumatic event when she was a small child, Cynthia had stopped loving herself. When she unraveled her pain all the way back to that point, she was able to recognize and view what happened to her from adult eyes. She was able to recognize where the threads had gone wrong and to rework them, this time with love, understanding, and acceptance.

Pouncing On the Positive Threads

Negative threads have a way of weaving into your life with very little effort. They are simply part of your world. Picking those threads out is very helpful. It is also helpful to pack your life with so many good and positive things there isn't much room left for anything else. Knowing this, you must be very intentional in pouncing on the positive threads that abound each day and making sure to weave them tightly into your life and thought life.

This is similar to growing a healthy green lawn. The positives in life are the blades of grass. The negatives in life are the weeds. In order to grow a healthy green lawn, you need to remove the weeds, but you also need to fertilize the grass. When the grass is fertilized, it fills in the holes left by the weeds. The thicker the grass, the harder it is for the weeds to get a foothold. Your life is kind of like that; the more positives you grab a hold of and integrate into your life, the harder it is for those stray negatives to find a place to land.

Some of you will complain that there is very little positive in your life to grab on to. This may be because you've stored up so much pain that there isn't room in your life or heart for much else. Focusing on the negatives often blinds you to seeing the positives. So, be patient with yourself and start small. Start by recognizing there are positives in this world. The apostle John says, "From the fullness of his grace we have all received one blessing after another" (John 1:16).

It is all too easy in life to see the negatives, to concentrate on the frustrations, problems, challenges, irritations, and annoyances. Sometimes, it can seem as if these are the only things that come your way. But the positives are often hidden beneath the clamor of the negative and must be looked for and focused on.

This was something Julie needed to learn how to do. Growing up, Julie had learned from her parents that she was not special. In fact, she had been told on multiple occasions that she was a "mistake." She'd heard her parents refer to her that way many times to other people, usually accompanied by laughter; she was the "mistake baby," born long after her parents thought they were through having children. Julie always felt like she was in the way of her parents' jobs and activities. They would often remark that they were "too old" or "too tired" and often used this as an excuse to distance themselves from her life. Living as an only child for most of her childhood because her siblings were grown and gone from the house, she had only herself for company. She struggled in school, unlike her older, smarter siblings. Naturally shy, she tended to blend into her surroundings, instead of standing out like her sister and brother, who appeared to excel in whatever they did. No, Julie wasn't special, and she learned not to expect anything special happening to her.

In order for Julie to break free of this shell of mediocrity she placed around herself, she needed to start seeing the positives in her life. She needed to start seeing herself as a positive in this world, instead of some sort of neutral. When Julie was first asked to list some of the positives in her life, she could hardly come up with any. On the flip side, she really didn't identify many negatives either. Julie had developed a bunker mentality—she just sort of existed hunkered down in neutral, neither exposed to painful negatives nor open to joyful positives. She needed to go ahead and poke her head up above the edge of her numbness and experience the world. Her assignment was to come up out of her shell and concentrate on the positives. She was to be alert and watchful for them. When something positive occurred or a positive thought broke through to her mind, she was to pounce on it! The more positives she pounced on, integrating them into her life and thought life, the more positives she saw.

You can be like Julie and learn to pounce on the positives. As John says, these blessings are real and out there and available for you to grab on to (John 1:16). Hold each positive up to the light; think about it. Meditate on it. Allow it to fill your mind and thoughts. Like Mary, treasure it in your heart.

By doing this, do you realize you are actually thinking about and meditating on God and his character? God is the source of all good, all positive, in this world. By focusing always on the negative and disbelieving the positive, you devalue the power of God in your life. God is not powerless to provide your life with positives. Did you know God refers to himself as "Almighty" more than three hundred times in the Bible? God is not just powerful, he is Almighty, and that includes over your life and thoughts.

Treat Yourself Gently

Proverbs 15:1 says, "A gentle answer turns away wrath, but a harsh word stirs up anger." I have most often heard this verse referenced when speaking about how you are to treat other people. With all the couples' work I've done over the years, I certainly believe it to be true! A gentle answer has a way of diffusing tense situations. On the other hand, when two people are itching for a fight, nothing will get one going quicker than a harsh verbal exchange. This proverb is absolutely true when it comes to how you deal with other people.

I'd like you to think, however, about this verse in the context of how you treat yourself. You have a relationship with yourself, just like you do with other people, and this relationship is manifested in your thought life. This thought life is what you say in your head as you carry on the course of your life. It is how you interpret what goes on around you. If your thought life springs from a well of bitterness, from a storehouse of wrongs you've kept record of, your thoughts will be negative, toward yourself, toward life, toward others.

What would happen instead if you chose to employ Proverbs 15:1 on yourself? What would happen if, instead of berating yourself, you loved yourself? What would happen if, instead of remembering every injury, every slight, you treated yourself gently and protected yourself? What would happen if, instead of tapping into your anger and inciting yourself to rage, you defused the anger? Wouldn't you be a much happier, less angry person?

Ethan and Emily cast a quick glance at each other, simultaneously communicating both dread and hope. It was a long shot, asking for the markers, but Ethan had blurted out the request and Emily had wholeheartedly agreed before either had known what they were doing. Now, it was up to their mother, Rachel, to respond.

Taking a deep breath and thinking a minute, she said slowly, "Well, those are really nice markers. I can understand why you'd want to have them."

Ethan went on to explain, with all the persuasion and earnestness of a ten-year-old, why they would be just perfect for all the drawing he was doing in class and how nice it would be to have more colors to draw with. He promised to bring them home from school whenever Emily wanted to use them. Rachel was a little surprised. She'd never heard Ethan mention how much he liked to draw before. Emily just kept nodding her head, happy to agree to whatever Ethan wanted.

"I hadn't planned on getting anything extra this trip, so we won't be able to get them today," Rachel said, to Ethan's obvious disappointment. "But, now that I know they mean so much to you, I'll see what I can do about planning for them the next trip."

"Maybe I could ask Grandma if there are some jobs I could do for her, to help pay for them," Ethan remarked, standing up a little straighter.

"I can help too," Emily insisted, wanting to be part of whatever Ethan was doing.

"That would be wonderful," Rachel replied. "Let's see what we can do together to help get those markers the next time we go shopping. We know right where they are and where to find them when we're ready."

Ethan and Emily nodded, and they continued on with the shopping. Rachel smiled as she listened to the two of them devising ever grander schemes for coming up with the money for the markers. She loved it when the kids got along and wanted to work together. It was so different from what she'd experienced growing up.

When Ethan had first asked for the markers, she'd been ready to snap back in irritation. It seemed like she always had to say no instead of yes, even about small things like markers. Except, she realized, the markers weren't a small thing to Ethan. She'd have to pay more attention to his art and drawing.

Inside, she sighed. There were so many things she just wasn't able to do because of her current financial situation, and it was a pretty stressful time. But the markers didn't really cost that much. With a little creativity, she could come up with the money to pay for them and, if the kids pitched in, it would be a good lesson and make those markers even more special to them.

At first, she'd wanted to scold them for always asking for things. But, truthfully, they were just kids and they really didn't ask for that much. They had no idea what it was like to have to stretch a dollar and keep track of every purchase. It wasn't their fault things were tight. It wasn't their fault a harmless question about markers had tapped into her feelings of insecurity and frustration. She refused to give in to the old familiar feeling of hopelessness that things would never get better. Her life was better, and two of the most important reasons for that were walking right beside her, chatting non-stop. She was so proud of them and the joy they brought to her life. Together, they'd get through this.

Note to Self

Because you live in a fallen world, you will have a record of wrongs. Paul doesn't say there is no record, he advises you not to *keep* that record. You'll see how to do that in more detail in later chapters. For right now, I want you to acknowledge you have kept, you have held on to, a record of wrongs.

Going back as far as you can remember, think about what is on your list. How have you been wronged in the past? I want you to be specific—naming names and identifying places. It is not enough to say, "People have always taken advantage of me." I want you to say, "When I was twelve years old my sister wore my new red blouse even though I told her she couldn't. She wore it and ruined it and then blamed me in front of my mother." The broad statement that people have always taken advantage of you didn't spring into your mind one day without reason. There are specific reasons. I want you to write them down.

Take as much time and paper as you need to do this exercise. At The Center, when people come to work in our intensive programs, one of the things we ask them to do is write down a time line of their life, including all of the significant events. We allow them to tell us what they consider to be significant. These lists are usually several pages long and often many, many pages long. This is how I want you to view this assignment. Write out your record of wrongs as a sort of time line. Take your time and open yourself up to the wrongs you're harboring.

For some of you, this will be extremely uncomfortable. You've been taught that it's wrong to harbor anger against anyone and will be reluctant to admit to these feelings. So, if this is you, I want you to write down *events*, things that have happened to you, that caused you pain or injury. You don't have to enter a judgment about the person or people involved or whether or not you've forgiven them. This isn't meant as an indictment against certain people in your life. Rather, it's a time line. Just say what happened to you.

For some of you, this will be uncomfortable because you've excused away the pain you feel over the past by complimenting yourself on how "adult," how "rational" you are now. Admitting to these things may seem like a step backward. Childish pain is still painful; in some ways, childish pain is the most intense. Willing it away does not make it go away. Only by taking it out and examining the pain can you place it into context and, as an adult, gain relief. If this exercise makes you feel like a hurt child again, don't flinch from it. Instead, move *toward* these feelings when they occur. Then, write them down so you can finally deal with them.

Now, I'd like all of you to go over your lists and create a shortened version. This is like a shorthand list that has all the highlights without the longer explanations. I'd like you to take this shortened version and look for any patterns of wrongs in your life. Perhaps there is some hurt or injury that keeps happening to you over and over again. These patterns can become the basis for more in-depth work, either alone or with professional assistance.

Next, I want you to take your list and indicate which wrongs you've "gotten over" and which ones you continue to ruminate on. Really think about each to determine which category you think they fall into. Don't necessarily go with your first thought but examine how you really feel. You may think you've "gotten over" something that's happened to you but realize with more thought it continues to affect you today.

Finally, I want you to come up with at least one reason why you've either "gotten over" a wrong or why you continue to hold on to that wrong. This is the list I'd like you to transfer here:

Why I've Gotten Over Wrongs

1.
2.
3.
4.
5.

You could say things like:

- It's not worth the pain to keep thinking about it.
- That person is out of my life now, so what's the use?
- I've grown up and moved on with my life.
- We were kids when that happened and we've both grown up.
- I've come to accept that's just the way this person is and they're never going to change.

There will be some wrongs on your list that you've held on to. They are fresh in your mind and affect you in a real-time way. These are wrongs you have not released. I want you to put down a reason why:

Why I've Held On to Wrongs

1.
2.
3.
4.
5.

You might put down:

- That person's never apologized or shown any remorse.
- I'm not going to let it happen to me again.

- It still makes me mad to think about it.
- What happened to me was so unfair I can't get over it.
- I'm not going to let that person off the hook.

The purpose of this exercise is not for you to provide "appropriate" or "acceptable" answers. I want you to be honest, even if it's difficult to express or admit. You are continuing your work to uncover the truth in your life. There is a reason why you've put some of these wrongs in the "gotten over" column and why you've put some in the "held on to" category.

Now, I'd like you to go back and look at the list you wrote under "Why I've Gotten Over Wrongs." I want you to take a second look at what I wrote and then what you wrote. I wrote:

- It's not worth the pain to keep thinking about it.
- That person is out of my life now, so what's the use?
- I've grown up and moved on with my life.
- We were kids when that happened and we've both grown up.
- I've come to accept that's just the way this person is and they're never going to change.

These are not my words; they are paraphrases of the reasons I've heard women give for why they've "gotten over" something. In my experience, these reasons are rarely sufficient to truly get over wrongs. These women thought they'd "gotten over" wrongs but, upon examination, realized they'd just glossed over the wrongs, engaging in more wishful thinking. Instead of doing the deep work to really root out the wrong, deal with it, and remove it, they chose a sort of cover statement, a reason to cover over the real pain they still felt. I'd like you to examine each of my statements.

- *It's not worth the pain to keep thinking about it.* This statement admits the pain is still there, still effective. It speaks of an inability to deal with the pain and a desire for it to stop hurting if only you can stop thinking about it. The truth, however, is it still hurts and you do think about it.
- *That person is out of my life now, so what's the use?* This is not a statement of victory in releasing a wrong. It is a statement of defeat. Even though the person is out of your life, this statement says the pain is still present.
- *I've grown up and moved on with my life.* It is unrealistic to expect the mere advancing of age to right all wrongs, comfort all hurts, or heal all wounds. Grown-ups still feel the pain of childhood; hurts have a way of coming along for the ride into adulthood.
- *We were kids when that happened and we've both grown up.* I hear this one quite a bit, especially when women speak of the hurts and injuries experienced from siblings growing up. Relegating an event to a childhood past does not remove its sting in the present.
- *I've come to accept that's just the way this person is and they're never going to change.* This statement says you've come to accept the situation, not the person. It is not a statement of understanding or empathy but rather of judgment. This statement is a crack in the door for anger to find its way back into your heart.

I realize this is not an easy exercise. I applaud you for working through it and being open and honest with yourself. Before you finish up this section and move on to the next chapter, I'd like you to create another time line. Some of you may have included these events earlier, but many may not have. The wrongs spoken about in the previous exercise were those perpetrated against you by others. Now, I'd like you to concentrate on those times when you believe you've "wronged" yourself. Some women have a harder time letting go of these wrongs than those caused by others. These are also a record of wrongs that love says you need to let go.

Love is not only love of others, it is also love of self. In Leviticus 19, when God gives Moses what is known as the Ten Commandments, he says, "Do not seek revenge or bear a grudge against one of your people, but love your neighbor as yourself. I am the LORD" (v. 18). This is a commandment to love your neighbor, but it also presupposes that you love yourself. If you expand this verse out, it would go something like this: "Do not seek revenge or bear a grudge against yourself, but love yourself. In the same way, show this kind of love to your neighbor." God expects you to love yourself; he wants you to love yourself. It is the basis of your love for your neighbor. When you keep an extensive record of wrongs against yourself, you will become easily angered with yourself, and it will be difficult for you to show yourself love and harder for you to get along with other people.

The final exercise of this chapter is to identify the wrongs you harbor in your heart against yourself. I want you to write down and chronicle those times in your life when you've felt you've been less than you should have been, humiliated by what you've done, ashamed of your actions, or mortified by your behavior.

As hard as it is to forgive others, I've found it is often much harder to forgive yourself. Because it is so hard to forgive yourself, these "wrongs" can be some of the deepest and most difficult to uncover. In chapter 2, you read about the power that guilt, shame, and fear have over your life. The wrongs you harbor against yourself reek with this negativity. You may also discover a pattern between what you have trouble letting go in others and what you secretly harbor against yourself.

Write down about yourself what you've gotten over and what you're still holding on to. Start to become aware of patterns and how they affect the way you view yourself and others. Write down any insights you gain and use these as a springboard for further work. You're going to use these lists later, during the chapter on forgiveness. For right now, though, become aware of what constitutes your record of wrongs—brought about by others and by yourself.

Dear God, help me to know how much you love me. Help me to have the courage to follow your example of love and keep no record of wrongs. But first, help me to understand and know the true record of wrongs I've harbored in my heart. I need this truth to come out into the open. Give me the strength to swing wide the doors of my heart and let the light in. Give me the courage to face what's inside. Give me the insight to know how to weave back together the fabric of my life with your love. You make all things new, Father. Create in me a clean heart, O God, and renew my spirit, as your Word says.

5

What's Stress Got
to Do with It?

Do not be anxious about anything, but in everything, by prayer and petition, with thanksgiving, present your requests to God. And the peace of God, which transcends all understanding, will guard your hearts and your minds in Christ Jesus.

Philippians 4:6–7

Women today function in a variety of arenas. Or, put another way, women today are expert "jugglers," having learned to keep a variety of objects constantly up in the air. There's nothing quite like the "oooohhhhs" and the "aaaaahhhhs" of the crowd watching the show and marveling, *How does she do all that?* And there's nothing quite like the crash that happens when something gets dropped and all the balls come tumbling down.

Pamela sat alone downstairs in the darkened house, in an even darker mood. Her husband and kids were already upstairs, asleep in bed. It was going to be several hours before Pamela had the same luxury. Somehow, sensing her mood, the rest of the family sort of evaporated upstairs earlier in the evening, without so much as a "good night." Of course, Pamela had several times during the course of the evening complained about how much work she had left to do. No one in her family operated under the illusion it was going to be a "good night" for Pamela.

Frankly, she was exhausted, having been out already three times this week with evening functions. It was Thursday and she absolutely, positively had to get this presentation put together for work on Friday. Time had just flat run out; unfortunately, so had her energy. Pamela sat at her desk, exhausted, unmotivated, and furious that the world got to rest when she couldn't.

It seemed like everyone expected her to step in and solve every problem. No one ever asked what it cost her to do so. Her kids just expected their lunches to be made, their errands run, their after-school events attended, their homework helped with, their projects polished. Her husband just expected food in the house, dinner on the table, the laundry done, the house clean, and his sexual needs met. Her office just expected every task to be completed, every crisis averted, every overtime agreed to, every demand met with aplomb. What none of them took the time to realize was how draining all this was on Pamela.

Her husband kept telling her to "let some things go," as if she could. The work she did with the parent group at school was very important to her, as well as the things she did at church, but those things kept getting crowded out by all the other demands. It seemed as if the things she liked to do best always got rushed, and the things she really didn't like took up way too much time and energy. As she sat and fumed about her situation, tears began to threaten. That made her even madder. It was going to be a very long night.

Women today are under stress. Stress is defined as when a force presses on, pulls on, pushes against, compresses, or twists something else. Many women can completely relate. It seems like life itself is pressing in on them, pulling them one way, pushing against them another, compressing them and twisting their life upside down. Frankly, they feel *squished*.

The Pressure to Perform

I believe part of this has to do with the amount of responsibilities women shoulder today. Years ago, keeping a household and raising a family were considered to be a full-time job. When I was growing up, my mother was a stay-at-home mom, one of many. Today, that full-time job of home and family is still around, but it's been compounded by part-time or full-time work outside the home by the majority of women. This is a financial reality for many married women and a financial necessity for single women. If you add in any sort of civic, community, school, or religious commitments, time is compressed even further.

It is not my intention to wade into the Mommy Wars here, but merely to point out the pressure women today feel. The more responsibilities a woman has, the more her time must be fragmented to handle those responsibilities. Women today seem to run around with stopwatches in their heads, calculating how much they can get done in smaller and smaller increments of time.

Trisha was absolutely thrilled. The ride home in traffic had miraculously taken ten minutes less than usual. Ten minutes was like gold! She could pick up and sort through the mail while she finished listening to her voice mails, pop the wash from this morning into the dryer, load all of the breakfast dishes into the dishwasher, and print up the agenda for tonight's meeting before she left the house again. It was kind of pathetic, really, that her life had somehow developed into ten-minute increments, but, hey, she was busy and every second counted.

I know women who operate not in ten-minute increments but in thirty-second increments. I remember one who spoke of the stress she was under and how it affected her day. She became irritated and annoyed when her computer was "slow" to boot up at work, when it took thirty seconds to dry her hands with an air dryer in the women's restroom instead of quickly with a paper towel. She began to resent it when other people took too much time on voice mail or spoke with too many pauses during conversation. Each "waste" of time became more and more grating. Over time, she came to realize she viewed these "barriers" in her day as adversarial. She put pressure on herself to be "productive" literally every second. Anything or anyone that took more time than she deemed acceptable became a cause of stress to her. Because she was already operating under stress, each slowdown made her more and more angry. She resented every second wasted and was frustrated with anyone who got in the way of her tightly scripted schedule.

It is not, of course, possible to be 100 percent productive. In fact, putting yourself under that kind of stress is counterproductive. I asked her why she felt compelled to resent the time it took her to dry her hands in the bathroom, and she said it was because she had "so much to do." She complained about all the pressure at work and her workload. When I asked her if she really felt her employers begrudged her the time it took to go to the bathroom, she had to reply no.

What it really came down to was not her employer's expectation but her own. She had a deep need to perform. Her sense of self-worth and value derived more from what she was able to accomplish than who she was as a person. She equated her value with how much she was able to do. She did not want to feel valueless, so she strove to do more and more, until even trips to the bathroom were resented. This is a recipe for soul-sucking stress.

Under Siege

In Scripture, the word *stress* isn't used much, not at all in the old King James Version. In the New International Version, it's used twice and only once in this context. I'd like you to read over that verse; I'll warn you, it's not pretty, because it comes out of the book of Jeremiah and God is speaking about what would happen in the city of Jerusalem during the siege of the Babylonian army:

> I will make them eat the flesh of their sons and daughters, and they will eat one another's flesh during the stress of the siege imposed on them by the enemies who seek their lives.
>
> Jeremiah 19:9

At first, I didn't think this verse really applied, but the more I read it and thought about it, and thought about what stress does to women, the more application I began to see.

- Stress produces a siege mentality.
- When you are in a siege mentality, even desperate measures become acceptable.

- When you are under siege, everything is perceived as a life-and-death struggle.
- When you are under siege, those closest to you are often harmed the most.

Pamela, whom you met earlier, really felt under siege by the pressures of her life. Every task, every demand on her time—even those she agreed to—began to feel like an attack against her peace of mind, her emotional stability, her physical stamina. In order to cope with the stress, she began to consume her own family. Oh, she didn't actually eat them, but she allowed other things to *eat up* her time and energy that should have been theirs. The anger and resentment she felt at their "insensitivity" to her stress ate away her love for them. In her heart, she knew this was wrong, but because of the desperation of her siege mentality, she allowed it to continue day after day. Pamela developed an "us versus them" mentality, with all of the demands and commitments of her life relegated to the "them" category and the "us" being herself and her family. The longer this siege of pressure continued, the more the "us" was turning into just "me," just Pamela against the world. It was at this point she decided she needed to get some help.

Unrealistic Expectations

Earlier you read about the branch of anger that comes from unrealistic expectations. Living with a siege mentality is really living in the realm of unrealistic expectations for most women. Most women today are not under siege by life. Instead, they live in the midst of life, with all of its problems, shortcomings, hiccups, and bumps in the road. This is the reality of life. But, if you have an unrealistic expectation that life will have no problems or, at least, you shouldn't, then the problems, short-comings, hiccups, and bumps in the road can make you feel like you personally are under siege. This isn't about reality, it's about *perception*.

Do you remember the children's story of Chicken Little? She goes out for a stroll one day and winds up walking under a tree and being hit in the head by a falling acorn. Immedi-ately, Chicken Little decides, "The sky is falling! The sky is falling!" She proceeds to act under that perception, gathering up several of her friends to go to the king about this crisis. In the heat of the moment, Chicken Little and her friends are tricked and ultimately eaten by a clever fox they meet on the way to the king.

Chicken Little walked straight under the branch of Unre-alistic Expectations. When the acorn hit her head, she took it as a catastrophe. It wasn't a catastrophe; it was a natural event. Acorns fall from trees. She just happened to be hit by one. She could have said, "Ouch! I just got hit by that falling acorn!" and continued on with her walk. Instead, that acorn became "The sky is falling!"

I wonder how many times this happens for women. Unreal-istic expectations turn the acorns of problems, shortcomings, hiccups, and bumps in the road into catastrophes. When women are under stress, they perceive their life to be under siege. When their life is under siege and an acorn drops, to them the sky is falling. When the rest of the world (or the people around them or their families) don't see things that way and respond accord-ingly, these women become defensive, angry, and hostile. They feel underappreciated, overworked, and taken for granted. The more they feel this way, the more they resent it and the angrier they get.

When you feel under siege by stress, it can appear that others don't have it as badly as you do. It can appear as if your situation, your stress, your siege, is worse than anyone else's, but this is appearance, not truth. Problems, shortcomings, hiccups, and bumps in the road are not special to you; they are a part of the human condition. To think otherwise—and become bitter about it—is an unrealistic expectation. Listen to what Job says: "For hardship does not spring from the soil, nor does trouble sprout from the ground. Yet man is born to trouble as surely as sparks fly upward" (Job 5:6–7). Have you ever watched a fire burn outside? Sparks from that fire just naturally fly upward in the draft created by the heat of the fire compared to the relative coolness of the surrounding air. Sparks flying up is a natural occurrence, like acorns falling down. Problems are like sparks flying upward; they are a natural, common occurrence. You have not been singled out for this treatment; it is part of the package deal called being human.

Thought Life Under Siege

So, if dealing with difficulties, challenges, setbacks, and problems are just a part of life, how is it that you come to view yourself as being singled out to live under siege? In my experience, one reason is that while there's no siege in your life, a siege is taking place in your thought life.

Take two different women and a single unfortunate event, a minor traffic accident. Both women are on their way to work. After braking at a four-way stop, each starts through the intersection, fiddling with the radio knob. Each looks up, startled, to realize the car in front hasn't continued on down the road but is actually stopped. Both slam on their brakes but still end up hitting the car ahead. For one woman, this is an acorn; for the other, it's a catastrophe.

For the catastrophe woman, this is just terrible. Shaken, she pulls over to the side of the road, fuming at the incompetence of this driver to just stop dead in the middle of the road. How dare he put her in this situation! She's going to have to turn this in to her insurance company, and no matter what she says, it will be recorded as her fault because she was the person in the back. Her insurance rates are going to go through the roof. For all she knows, this guy will fake some sort of injury, even though she wasn't going very fast at all! She can't believe this is happening now, of all times. She just knows her hours are going to be cut back at work, and her rent was just raised two months ago. With the increased insurance rates, how is she going to manage to pay for it all? It's not like she can go to a different insurance company, because now she's got an accident on her record and no one will want to insure her. She'll be lucky if her insurance isn't cancelled and she isn't stuck paying whatever exorbitant rates her insurance company comes up with. Spitting mad and practically in tears, she gets out of her car, slamming the door, to survey the damage.

For the acorn woman, this accident is unfortunate. As she pulls over to the side of the road, she's just glad she wasn't going any faster! It was her fault for looking down at the radio and not paying attention to the car ahead of her. Hopefully, the damage won't be too bad, for either her car or the car ahead. Well, these things happen; she'll need to be more attentive next time. It could have been worse, so she's grateful it wasn't. She's embarrassed about hitting the man but determined to do the right thing as she gets out of her car to survey the damage.

The thought life of the first woman escalated this minor fender bender into a catastrophe. Within a matter of seconds, the accident morphed into a financial crisis, a case of medical fraud, and problems with her insurance company. In her mind, the catastrophe woman was yelling at herself, *The sky is falling!* This left her shaken, angry, and upset.

The thought life of the second woman diffused the situation and allowed this fender bender to remain in context. Within a matter of seconds, she was able to put it into perspective, recognize the positives in the situation, accept responsibility, and determine to do the right thing. In her mind, the acorn woman just told herself, *Ouch!* and continued on. This left her calm, prepared, and optimistic.

Two women—one situation. For the catastrophe woman, her thoughts were flying a mile a minute, splattering negativity all across her mind and emotions. For the acorn woman, her thoughts centered her, allowing her to deal with the situation in as positive a way as possible. The catastrophe woman lives under siege, controlled by her thought life, which compounds and magnifies every problem into a crisis. The acorn woman lives in control of her thought life, allowing her to intentionally respond to situations instead of merely reacting to them.

What kind of woman are you? Life is full of stresses, minor fender benders that happen every day in different arenas. There are acorns and then there are real catastrophes. How will you be prepared to weather a true catastrophe when it comes? You need to ask yourself if your thought life is your ally in times of trouble or if it has you under siege, even when things go well.

Letting Go of the Reins

I believe one reason women turn acorns into catastrophes is because you have so many responsibilities. Because you are responsible, you believe you should be in control. Stress is produced in your life when you feel out of control. The question you need to ask yourself is whether or not you really have control over any given situation and then act accordingly. As a woman, you have family responsibilities, but really you only have control over yourself. You can guide, teach, and influence, but other people in your family may and will act outside of your control. This is an acorn, not a catastrophe. As a woman, you have work responsibilities, but you really only have control over your work product. You can model, encourage, and motivate, but other people at your work may and will act outside of your control. This is an acorn, not a catastrophe. It is when you think that your responsibilities should give you control, and they don't, that you feel out of control and under stress. By learning to let go, you can reduce the amount of needless stress in your life.

At The Center, we use this guide for helping people let go of their need for control. Because the majority of those I counsel are women, it seems appropriate to include it here. (I encourage you to memorize and incorporate into your thought life any of these statements that particularly resonate with you.)

Letting Go

To "let go" does not mean to stop caring; it means I can't do it for someone else.

To "let go" is not to cut myself off; it's the realization that I can't control another.

To "let go" is not to enable, but to allow learning from natural consequence.

To "let go" is to admit powerlessness, which means the outcome is not in my hands.

To "let go" is not to care for, but to care about.

To "let go" is not to fix, but to be supportive.

To "let go" is not to judge, but to allow another to be a human being.

To "let go" is not to be in the middle arranging all of the outcomes, but to allow others to affect their own destinies.

To "let go" is not to be protective, it's to permit another to face reality.

To "let go" is not to deny, but to accept.

To "let go" is not to nag, scold, or argue, but instead to search out my own shortcomings and correct them.

To "let go" is not to adjust everything to my desires, but to take each day as it comes, and cherish myself in it.

To "let go" is not to regret the past, but to grow and live for the future.

To "let go" is to fear less and to love more.

Those women who have a high need for control live in a paradoxical world. If you are one of these women, you desire control in the people and world around you and experience a great deal of stress when you don't get it. The paradox is, while you desire control over others, you are not in control of yourself. You are not in control of yourself when you allow your thought life to run amok, spewing negativity and festering with unrealistic expectations. You are not in control of yourself when you allow yourself to build up resentment, anger, and frustration. You are not in control of yourself when you view acorns as catastrophes and demand that everyone else in your life view them the same way.

Worldview

Part of this may have to do with your particular worldview. Your thought life is often anchored to your worldview. When life is at odds with your worldview, it becomes out of joint and discordant, like a jangled note always ringing in your head that never resolves to its proper chord. Living this way is stressful and irritating in a physical, visceral way. Women often expose their worldview when speaking of the expectations they have about other people and life in general. This goes back, again, to unrealistic expectations. If your worldview is formed on the basis of unrealistic expectations, it will always seem out of place with whatever is going on around you. The harder you try to bring your life into control through the mechanism of your worldview, the more disappointed, angry, and frustrated you will be.

There are enough normal troubles in life, as you've read in Job. They are as natural as sparks flying upward. Troubles are stressful. When you manufacture catastrophes out of acorns, you increase the stress in your life. The more stress you experience, the more difficult it becomes to deal with that stress because of the toll it takes on you. The more overwhelmed you feel by the stresses in your life, the easier it is for anger, resentment, and bitterness to take root. Stress runs the gamut of negativity, from A to Z.

Anger—stress is painful, and pain produces anger

Blame—stress produces a siege mentality and makes you look for enemies to blame

Cynicism—stress poisons your positive attitude and magnifies the negatives leading to cynicism

Defensiveness—stress sends you over the edge, pushing back against anyone or anything that adds to your stress, resulting in a defensive posture

Edginess—stress emphasizes the fight-or-flight response, making you on constant alert for the next source of stress, leaving you living a life on edge

Frustration—stress that is perpetual grinds down your ability to be emotionally buoyant, leading to an attitude of frustration

Guilt—stress internalized leads to feelings of self-shame, blame, and guilt

Hopelessness—stress compounded over time wears down your optimism, producing a general sense of hopelessness about your life and situation

Irritability—stress causes all of your senses to be revved to the max, leading to irritability

Judgmental—stress creates tunnel vision, focusing people and events through a self-made filter, producing a narrow, judgmental view

Know-It-All—stress produces a desperate desire for control in order to relieve or manage the stress, increasing the need for you to be right so you can be more in control

Lashing Out—stress produces anger, which makes you vulnerable to lashing out to others in anger

Martyrdom—stress and its tunnel vision can make you feel as if no one else suffers the way you do

Nervousness—stress and the strain it produces can make you wary of where the next stress will come from, increasing your nervousness

Out of Control—stress leaves little room for reflection, recovery, or recouping, making you feel adrift and that your life is out of control

Panic—stress and the out-of-control feeling it causes can produce a deep sense of panic over what in the world will happen to you next

Quick Tempered—stress and the pressure-cooker environment it generates make you quick-tempered and reactionary

Resentment—stress is a uniquely personal experience, leaving you vulnerable to feelings of resentment that others don't feel the way you do

Stewing—stress is relentless, an unwelcome companion that intrudes upon your mind and thought life, demanding constant attention

Tension—stress heightens your senses, your feelings of danger, causing increased tension

Unrealistic Expectations—stress and unrealistic expectations are the chicken and the egg; no matter which comes first, negativity is unleashed

Volatility—stress causes feelings of catastrophe, where anything can happen, resulting in a volatile, unstable world

Worrying—stress accumulated from yesterday and present today cause worry about tomorrow

e**X**tremes—stress and the siege mentality pave the way for extreme behavior as a desperate response

Yelling—stress leaves little room for a peaceful or calm response but an open door to rage and anger

Zero Energy—stress drains your battery and leaves you running, still running, on empty

God the Spotter

Please realize I am not condemning all stress in life as negative. On the contrary, some stress, some "pushing against," is beneficial. It is how you get stronger. This is stress that is well managed. This kind of stress is like a weight lifter who "pushes against" weight to become stronger. It is important with stress, then, that you lift it properly. In order to lift it properly, you need to have a "spotter." In a weight room, a spotter is the person who helps you prepare to handle the weight and is right there with you, to assist if you get into trouble. God is like your spotter. He does not remove all "weight" from you but works with you, knowing you, to build you up and make you stronger.

Some of you aren't happy about lifting any weight. It all seems too heavy and burdensome. Instead of assuming you can't handle the weight, perhaps you should take a lesson from the apostle Paul, who said of the "weight" in life: "[1] Therefore, since we have been justified through faith, we have peace with God through our Lord Jesus Christ, [2] through whom we have gained access by faith into this grace in which we now stand. And we rejoice in the glory of God. [3] *Not only so, but we also rejoice in our sufferings, because we know that suffering produces perseverance; [4] perseverance, character; and character, hope.* [5] And hope does not disappoint us because God has poured out his love into our hearts by the Holy Spirit, whom he has given us" (Rom. 5:1–5, emphasis added).

I put the italics and verse numbers in this passage because I'd like you to continue to think about dealing with stress with God's help like lifting weights. To me, verses 1 and 2 are like getting yourself set to take the weight of life by reminding you about the truth of your standing with God. Then, verses 3 and

4 speak about the heavy lifting you do as you bear up under the weight of sufferings. Verse 5 is like the spotter who helps your hands guide the weight back to the weight stand. He does this by reminding you of all the positives to be gained after you've borne the weight of suffering.

When you try to lift the load and stresses of this life by yourself, it's bound to leave you exhausted, empty, resentful, and angry. God has shown his mercy and desire to be there for you, amidst these stresses, these "struggles." If you've been struggling with these stresses and burdens by yourself, it's time to call in your heavenly spotter.

Some of you may be so weary that you desire for all struggles to cease, all burdens to be lifted. This, again, is an unrealistic expectation, and Jesus debunks this wishful thinking in John 16:33 by reminding you, "In this world you will have trouble. But take heart! I have overcome the world." He also says, "Come to me, all you who are weary and burdened, and I will give you rest. Take my yoke upon you and learn from me, for I am gentle and humble in heart, and you will find rest for your souls. For my yoke is easy and my burden is light" (Matt. 11:28–30). There are troubles in this world and there is a yoke for you to bear, either the world's or Christ's. Christ is compassionate, loving, and gentle; the world is seldom so.

Note to Self

It's time to personalize all this talk about stress and figure out what causes stress in your life. Over my years in counseling, I've been fascinated how individualized stress really is. Do you remember the example I gave of the catastrophe woman and the acorn woman each handling the fender-bender differently? I have found that to be true over and over again, with different types of stresses. One woman will weather the stress calmly and the other will be blown over and uprooted by it. In order to strengthen your ability to handle stress, it's important to know which ones you can handle and which ones you can't.

I'd like you to start by listing the stresses in your life, putting them in either the Acorn or the Catastrophe category. In the Acorn category, put those stresses you feel you do pretty well handling. Really think about your list. It can be as varied as getting cut off on the freeway to dealing with your mother-in-law. From navigating the family budget to managing a chronic health condition. Come up with an Acorn List. Try for ten:

Acorn List

1.
2.
3.
4.
5.
6.
7.
8.
9.
10.

Now, come up with your Catastrophe List. These are the stresses in your life that really bog you down. You feel overwhelmed by them. When they happen to you, they knock you for a loop. These are the stresses that really make you angry. If you have a stress in your life that you spend a great deal of time ruminating about, write it down under the Catastrophe column. If it was really no big deal, you wouldn't be spending so much time and energy thinking about it. Again, this is your list. It is appropriate for you to put down other people and how their actions or attitudes affect you. Open yourself up to the truth of your anger over these stresses in your life.

Catastrophe List

1.
2.
3.
4.
5.
6.
7.
8.
9.
10.

For fairness, I've included space for ten in this Catastrophe List. You may or may not have that many. (If you've listed five or more, however, I heartily encourage you to consider working with a therapist or counselor to address them. The wear-and-tear on your whole person—your emotions, relationships, physical body, and spiritual self—is no doubt significant and should be addressed. You don't need to live this way, being overwhelmed by these stresses. Consider that now is the time to get help.)

Next, I'd like you to go back over each list. Next to each item under your Acorn and Catastrophe lists, I want you to think about one or two things you say to yourself when that particular stress occurs in your life. This exercise speaks to your thought life and what you tell yourself that either diffuses or escalates the stress. Once you've done this, I want you to transfer those thoughts under either Diffuse or Escalate below:

Diffuse

1.
2.
3.
4.
5.
6.
7.
8.
9.
10.

Escalate

1.
2.
3.
4.
5.
6.
7.
8.
9.
10.

I'd like you to begin using the best and most effective tools under your Diffuse list on some of those Catastrophes you've listed. You know these are effective for you and help you diffuse other sorts of stress, so give them a try on those stresses that continue to present a problem to you.

As for those things you say to yourself, that escalate your stress, these I'd like you to take time to examine. For each escalating thought, answer the following.

- How long have I felt this way?
- Why do I believe this to be true?
- If I don't believe it to be true, why do I act as if it is?
- Why does this thought have such power over me?
- Is there anything about this thought that I want or need to be true?
- What would happen to my life and my thought life if this thought wasn't true?
- What positive steps can I take to protect myself from this escalating thought?
- Am I willing to release this thought from my life?

Lastly, give each and every escalating thought over to God, whether or not you're ready to release it. Pray specifically about each and ask God to strengthen you in those thoughts you are ready to release and help you to release the rest. Do this right now. Do this often. Do this every time one of these escalating thoughts invades your mind. Call on God's power and protection over you. Claim the renewal of your mind promised in Romans 12:2.

When you claim the renewal of your mind promised in Romans 12:2, you have control over your thought life. This is the true control that assists you in dealing with the stresses and struggles of life. Before you read my Letting Go statements earlier in the chapter, I asked you to pay attention and incorporate those that especially spoke to you into your thought life. Going back over that list, write down the three statements that touched a chord in your heart. Look for how these statements relate to either your Diffuse or your Escalate lists.

Letting Go

1.
2.
3.

These three statements are definitely items for prayer and meditation. Ask God to speak to you through these statements and reveal his truth for your life.

More and more, I've come to appreciate the power of praying Scripture. This is the practice of taking a passage of Scripture and applying it in prayer. Praying through Scripture and internalizing its truth will help you diffuse and deescalate the stresses that come into your life. Prayer itself is a calming, cleansing activity. Reading and meditating on God's Word helps you reset your spiritual compass. Remember the words of Christ—will you have trouble in this world? Yes! Don't forget, however, the rest of that verse—Christ has overcome this world of trouble.

To end this chapter, I'd like you to pray through Romans 8:35 and 8:37–39, because these verses speak directly to the power of Christ and the love of God to combat all of the stresses life throws your way.

Holy Father, I trust my life to you. I give all my stresses and struggles, my burdens and my cares over to you. For who shall separate me from the love of Christ? Shall trouble or hardship or persecution or famine or nakedness or danger or sword? Shall any of the things I am so fearful of or that affect me so negatively? No, dear God, I can conquer and have victory over all these things because of your Son who loves me. Please help me to be convinced that neither death nor life, neither angels nor demons, neither the present nor the future, nor any powers, neither height nor depth, nor anything else in all creation, will be able to separate me from your love that is in Christ Jesus my Lord. Grant me peace in my heart, strength in my mind, and courage in my soul as I face the stresses of my life. Help me to know that you are sovereign over my life, that I am your child, and that you love me so very much.

=== 6 ===

Why Shouldn't I Be Angry When Life Is Unfair?

Defend the cause of the weak and fatherless; maintain the rights of the poor and oppressed. Rescue the weak and needy; deliver them from the hand of the wicked.

Psalm 82:3–4

Historically, women have been oppressed. You've often been asked to carry too heavy a burden. You've been marginalized and patronized. You've been abused in any number of ways. These wounds are very real, very deep, and very damaging. The anger and rage that develop from this absolute affront to all that is right, decent, and fair in life can be immense—so immense, sometimes it overflows its banks and floods a woman's life.

Recently, the local newspaper has been following the story of a fourteen-year-old girl who was rescued from a home in a small town to the northeast of where I live. This teenager weighed less than fifty pounds, having been systematically abused by her stepmother, who kept food and water from her. Because of this girl's "behavioral problems," according to the stepmother, she was relegated to eating only toast and drinking only one half of a small Dixie cup of water per day. Her stepmother kept her locked up at night so she couldn't sneak out and get water. She monitored the girl when she took a shower and went to the bathroom so she didn't sneak water. Brushing her teeth was not allowed for the same reason.

As I read through the accounts of the discovery and rescue, the arrest and charging of the stepmother and the girl's father, who was aware of the abuse but did nothing, I was appalled at the suffering endured by this young girl and the depravity of the adults responsible. It made me outraged, and, sadly, the outrage was familiar.

In my line of work, I hear stories of women that literally keep me up at night. Often, I am the first person they've revealed their pain to in years, if ever. I have felt inside my heart and soul the horror and the hurt experienced by these women. Hearing their stories, I can appreciate the anger and rage they feel. Helping to bring some sense of relief, recovery, and restoration is why I show up for work every day. It is what helps me finally sleep at night. And then I wake up and read the morning newspaper.

Bad Things

This is a world of injustice. Bad things happen to the young, the innocent, the good. It is not fair; it is not just; it is not the world God intended. That world was broken by sin, and the world you live in now is an unjust world, a fallen world, where evil and wrongs abound. This brokenness, this evil, is now the reality. God meant for something completely different, and this change is a source of grief. In Genesis 6:5–6, Scripture records, "The LORD saw how great man's wickedness on the earth had become, and that every inclination of the thoughts of his heart was only evil all the time. The LORD was grieved that he had made man on the earth, and his heart was filled with pain." God's heart fills with pain at evil, including the evil that happens to you.

As you read in the last chapter, this world is one of trouble. Some of that trouble will come about through circumstances and events, with no evil intent. Sadly, some of that trouble surely comes through the evil intent of others. Scripture calls this oppression. Oppressing the poor and weak is one thing that makes God very angry, as you saw in chapter 1.

What does God do with his anger over oppression? Because he is God, it has motivated him to wipe out entire nations. The Old Testament is full of examples of nations who oppressed others and paid the consequence of utter annihilation. In Jeremiah, God's intentions are clear: "'But if any nation does not listen, I will completely uproot and destroy it,' declares the LORD" (Jer. 12:17). For some of you deeply wounded by evil, wickedness, sin, and injustice, you want to mete out this kind of scorched-earth policy against your oppressors. The depth and intensity of your rage demands nothing less. I can understand that sentiment and have felt it well up in myself at times.

There are times for this kind of cleansing anger that burns away all ties between the oppressed and the oppressor. However, in the conflagration that comes from this kind of anger, I have rarely found the damage confined only to the responsible party. Others often get caught up and burned in the process. The initial harm done by the oppressor is in the past, but it is followed by an angry aftermath that continues to perpetrate harm long after the original oppressor is gone. If this is true of your own life and experience, it is time to put an end to this type of anger.

Jenny listened to the voice message from Colin with mixed emotions. Part of her wanted to smile at how sweet he sounded over the phone. The other part of her counseled to avoid being swayed by the sound of his voice. She had already made up her mind not to continue going out with him. Her reasons were very specific and justified. He wasn't serious enough. He lacked motivation. He wasn't sensitive enough to her needs. For each reason, she could relive a detailed example of that failing.

While at first his message made her smile a little inside, now it just made her angry. She was going to have to be blunt and tell him not to call her anymore. It was just so frustrating. It wasn't fair! Why couldn't she find the right type of man? Didn't they exist on the planet anymore? She was beginning to wonder.

A small tendril of despair threatened to creep into her thoughts, but she quickly banished it away with the force of her own convictions. She would never, ever be taken advantage of by any man again. If she set a high bar, it was for her own protection. It was better this way. Until the right man came along, she determined to stand guard over herself and not let anyone in. As she thought this to herself, Jenny felt bars of anger drop down over her heart. They felt familiar and safe. Not again, not ever.

When bad things happen to you, the effects cast ripples over the surface of your life. Intense anger can radiate out from a traumatic event. You have already read the adjectives used for anger that speak to its power and fury. Anger this powerful can be termed rage, a violent and uncontrolled anger. This kind of anger does not stop at the threshold of common sense or compassion or even truth. Rather, fueled by the horror, injustice, and oppression of bad things, it consumes everything in its path. In doing so, this kind of rage causes damage of its own, apart from whatever damage was caused by the initial event or circumstances.

Collateral Damage

Sometimes a woman will come to work with me in the midst of a traumatic, oppressive circumstance. More often, however, the work we will do together happens after the fact. The wound, the abuse, the trauma—the descriptors are as horrific and varied as the events themselves—are rooted in the past, but she continues to experience painful repercussions in the present. Perhaps one of the most significant repercussions is a loss of trust. She does not truly trust anything but her anger. Only her anger seems pure and right and unequivocal. It is at this point when she grafts her identity as a person onto her anger. The reason for her anger and the anger itself become the defining characteristic of her life and reality. Therefore, its power over her is incredibly difficult to diminish. The injustice behind her anger colors every other situation in which she finds herself. Without meaning to, she has chained herself to her monster.

That phrase may sound vaguely familiar to you. Earlier I talked about Cynthia Rowland-McClure, who wrote the book about bulimia *The Monster Within*. At a young age, Cynthia was traumatically burned over the bottom part of her body. In the hospital, she received medical care that was scarring but necessary, from professionals who were proficient but insensitive.

As an adult, she equated the treatment she received with the violation of a rape. A monstrous anger began to form within Cynthia as a young girl. As a teenager, this building rage took on the face of bulimia and became her monster within.

Anger can also become a monster within. This monster usually attacks one of two ways—either it attacks inward, creating a deep, debilitating depression, or it attacks outward, in a blasting flame of rage.

Victimization

Along with tying your identity to your anger, there is also a temptation to define yourself as a victim: once a victim, always a victim. This negative, fatalistic approach has its perceived positives. If you consider yourself a victim, you have a familiar template with which to evaluate yourself and your life. You can demand redress from others. You can remove any responsibility you have as an oppressor yourself. In this self-definition, you are always wounded, always entitled, always justified, always angry.

There is deep pain in being victimized by circumstances or people. This is a wounding event, a defining moment. The intensity of the trauma burns an image onto your life. To think otherwise would be to enter into the realm of denial, which is damaging and unhealthy in its own right. Instead, you need to integrate the bad things that happened to you into who you are; they are a part of you, a part of your experience. However, when you integrate victimization into your view of yourself, you grant authority and control over your life and your future to the worst thing that's ever happened to you.

When you say "once a victim, always a victim," this becomes a self-fulfilling prophecy. I understand the perverse comfort to be found in knowing what will happen next, especially if you've been hurt. If you decide, based on the past, that bad things will always happen to you, then at least you can be prepared. You're ready, you're on alert; you're on guard. You are also anxious and defensive. On the constant lookout for bad things, you will find them.

Once you decide to look at life through this victim filter, you intentionally make yourself color-blind. You will be able to detect every insult, every injury, every heartache, every dismissal. Looking through this lens, you will cease to recognize the subtle shades of remorse, regret, and repentance and be blind to the circumstantial and the unintentional. Once this vision is lost, you compromise your ability to experience kindness, joy, gentleness, genuine delight. These emotions, though rich and rooted deep, are often scorched away like stubble in the burning heat of anger. Though not gone completely, it can take a long time for them to break through to the surface of your life again.

Once you have declared yourself a victim, it is an easy step to cross over into the concept of entitlement. After all, you are a victim, you have been wounded; you hurt and have needs that arise out of that woundedness. Therefore, because of this condition of crisis, it is your right to ask others to redress your pain. If you ask and they do not deliver, then you are justified in demanding. Your need for redress trumps any of their needs. You feel justified demanding your needs be met before anyone else's, whether that person is responsible for your pain or not.

When your behavior in your own mind becomes justified by your victimhood, you remove any responsibility you might have for becoming an oppressor yourself. This allows your anger and rage to have free rein over you and those around you. This becomes your "get out of jail free" card when it comes to perpetrating your own bad behavior. In this mode, other people become mere objects of your anger. When people become objects, oppression thrives. Often, those who become objects of your wrath are those you love the most—your family, your friends, your spouse, your children. Behavior you would never exhibit toward business or social acquaintances is freely expressed in private. The people who know your pain best and are the least responsible for it can become the ones you turn to most for redress. This is also living an unfair life; you now are being unfair to others. Injustice comes full circle.

Depression

Because many women were taught not to express anger, their anger has nowhere else to go but inward. When anger is suppressed, when it is bottled up and not allowed to be expressed, the built-up pressure is enormous. In order to escape the mounting pressure, some women choose to turn off their anger completely. They go into a numbing mode, hoping to be rid of their anger. If you are depressed, this numbing settles in as a wet, gray blanket over you, slowly suffocating the range of your emotional life. It can seem a reasonable trade—no more anger for no more emotions.

Depression is a fatalistic response to anger. Depression assumes the worst and acts accordingly. When you are depressed, there is no end in sight, no one who understands, no one who can help. At some point, even trying to come out of the depression is too strenuous, as all your energy is sapped from constantly living with a lid on your emotions. When you live with depression, what energy you have does not spring from life, it springs from anger. Paradoxically, the very thing you reject—your anger—is the one thing fueling that rejection. You cannot see any way out, so in your anger you decide there isn't a way out to find in the first place.

Depression is just another way of holding things in secret. Depression says that nothing matters, so nothing is ever discovered, discussed, worked through, and moved beyond. Depression says if there is no use, then what's the point? So, the bad things stay secret, hidden underneath the cover of apathy and despair. They are secret, however, but never static. When the hidden things threaten to break through your apathy, you may find yourself drawn to self-medicating, self-numbing behaviors.

It is no surprise to me that many women choose depression as a way to cope with anger. After all, many of you as children learned to suppress the anger you felt, it being neither appropriate nor permissible. In this type of upbringing, you probably also learned to keep things secret. The bad things you saw and experienced within the family were to be buried. The goal was to appear to be perfect on the outside, so all the bad things got swept away, out of sight. The appearance was more important than the reality, the surface things over the truth. There comes a point at which, however, there simply isn't any more room in which to stuff things, and those bad things start bulging out.

And so goes the ripple effect of bad things. What hurt you back then continues to affect you right now. And the very people God intended to help salve your wounds and comfort your heart are either locked out through the bars of depression or relegated to the position of servicing your rage. What you really want is to proclaim the truth of your anger. What you want is justice. In order to get that justice, you may need to step out of the way with your anger and let God take the lead.

Upholding Justice

The evil committed by one person against another has always and will always grieve God. He is not unaware of your situation. He is not oblivious to what happened to you. Because bad things exist in this world does not mean God condones them. He will act according to his time, which is not always yours or mine.

Perhaps you think it is totally up to you to exact justice for the injustice perpetrated against you. If so, listen to what the prophet Isaiah says in Isaiah 30:18: "Yet the LORD longs to be gracious to you; he rises to show you compassion. For the LORD is a God of justice. Blessed are all who wait for him!" Listen also to what God says through the prophet Ezekiel in Ezekiel 34:16: "I will search for the lost and bring back the strays. I will bind up the injured and strengthen the weak, but the sleek and the strong I will destroy. I will shepherd the flock with justice." God is a God of justice; this is important to him. Because you must wait for justice does not mean it will never come. For many women who wait for justice, anger becomes their constant companion. Over time, their anger becomes more important than justice. Over time, being angry becomes a form of justice.

If you want justice, your anger is not going to secure it for you. Only a judge, the true Judge, can secure it for you. In Deuteronomy 32:35 God promises, "It is mine to avenge; I will repay." In case that last statement isn't clear enough, here is how the apostle Paul puts it in Romans 12:19: "Do not take revenge, my friends, but leave room for God's wrath, for it is written: 'It is mine to avenge; I will repay,' says the Lord."

It may simply not be within your power to demand, let alone receive, justice from the person who harmed you. If you determine to stay angry until justice is done and restitution received, you may have a very, very long time to wait. Instead, I suggest you acknowledge your anger and give it to God to carry for you since he is already aware of and grieved by it. You are not the only one angered over what was done to you. Leave room, as Paul says, for God's wrath.

When you give up your anger to God, asking him to give you justice, you join a veritable host of others who have done the very same thing. From Abel in the Old Testament, whose blood cried out to God from the ground in Genesis 4:10, to Stephen in the New Testament, who was stoned and as he died said, "Lord, do not hold this sin against them" (Acts 7:60). God is the only one capable of dealing with the strength of your anger. Left within you, it will continue to cause you damage and harm those you love. You may feel that the expanse of your rage is so large, nothing can contain it. However, God is as big as the universe and beyond. He is big enough, powerful enough, trustworthy enough for you to turn over your anger.

As destructive as anger can be, some women struggle to give it up. When the anger becomes the basis of who you are and how you interpret life, you can feel naked, exposed, and vulnerable without it. You can be fearful and think to yourself, *Who will I be without it?* Again, it is the same principle for those with an addiction; as terrible as it is, you are afraid of what life will be like without it. In order to give up your addiction or your anger, you need to learn other ways of coping with the world.

God understands your anger, but he does not want you to turn it into an idol. Anger becomes your idol when you turn to it to find your identity, when you turn to it to give you solace and comfort, when you turn to it and give your time, your thoughts, your energy, and your devotion over to your anger. God wants to be how you cope and deal with the world. God wants you to lay your anger down and turn to him instead.

I understand what a difficult concept this is, especially if you've been living with your anger for a long time. You have developed complicated and compassionate rationales for holding on to your anger. Even though you trust in God, you also trust in your anger. If you are truthful, even though you worship God, you also worship your anger. This is unacceptable to God. He demands that you worship him alone: "Do not worship any other god, for the LORD, whose name is Jealous, is a jealous god" (Exod. 34:14). If only the people of Israel had taken this truth to heart, they could have avoided untold heartache. Their example is provided in Scripture so you don't have to take the same path.

Instead, give up your anger—all your anger—to God. There isn't a small piece of it you're entitled to hang on to. Again, Ephesians 4:31 says, "Get rid of all bitterness, rage and anger, brawling and slander, along with every form of malice." This verse says *all*. It doesn't differentiate whether or not that rage is justified. This verse is not phrased in the form of a suggestion; it is a command.

Angry at God

How do you turn your anger over to God, however, when he's the object of your anger? In the midst of your oppression, you may have cried out to God for help but felt there was none forthcoming. You may have wondered why God allowed such a bad thing to happen to you. You may ask yourself why you were not protected better or protected at all. Because you know and understand God is sovereign, you may assign him a measure of responsibility for the bad things done by others against you.

There will also be some of you reading this book who have undergone traumatic circumstances where no oppressor or perpetrator was involved. You may have experienced the death of a loved one, be dealing with a chronic or terminal illness, or have suffered through a catastrophic event or natural disaster. Within the midst of this trauma, there was no face of an "enemy" to focus on. Can you be angry at the winds that ripped your house apart or the cancer cells that claimed the life of your loved one? Can you be angry at the fire that devastated your home or the miscarriage that stole the promise of your unborn child? Sometimes when people are overwhelmed by events outside of human control, they look to God for answers. More than answers, they look to God for reasons. In their anger and pain, they turn their faces to heaven and cry out, "Why?" They are angry at God for causing the catastrophe; they are angry at God for not intervening to prevent it.

Are you angry at God? As a Christian, you may find it difficult to express anger at God or even to admit you harbor any. If it was frowned upon for you to show anger growing up, it may have been considered a mortal sin to show anger at God. How do you go to God with your anger when he's the one you're really mad at?

The only way I know of is to just be honest. If you are angry at God, how can you suppose he isn't already aware of your anger? Do you suppose you are the only person who's ever been angry with him? If you do, you haven't read through the Psalms lately. In Psalm 6:3, David cries out, "My soul is in anguish. How long, O Lord, how long?" In Psalm 13:1–2, he says, "How long, O Lord? Will you forget me forever? How long will you hide your face from me? How long must I wrestle with my thoughts and every day have sorrow in my heart? How long will my enemy triumph over me?" In Psalm 35, David begins a recitation of the injustices of his situation and then asks in verse 17, "O Lord, how long will you look on?"

Yet, with all of that crying out, with all of his anger and frustration, God still calls David his "chosen one" (Ps. 89:3). God does not reject David because David is often angry at him. Even though David expresses his anger and frustration at God, David always comes back around to the central fact that God loves him. He doesn't always understand how that love works within all of the bad things that happen to him, but in the end he always chooses to trust in God's love. Trusting God's love, in the face of struggles, problems, and pain, is an act of faith.

The Bible calls David God's "chosen one," anger and all. Did you know you are also God's chosen one? He has chosen to love you, to comfort you, to save you. He knows how many days you have on this earth, how many hairs you have on your head, your innermost thoughts including your anger. Because of what you've been through, you may not feel very "chosen." If you feel "chosen" at all, you may feel chosen for disaster. This is a common sentiment expressed by those who have lived through a traumatic event or circumstances.

Even if you are angry with God, he is still the only place for you to go. The effects of what you've experienced—the pain and the anger—may have left you feeling empty and depleted. If this is you, listen to the words of the Old Testament prophet

Habakkuk, who unflinchingly chronicles the state of his own despair over the catastrophes he has witnessed in his life. In Habakkuk 3:17–18, he concludes with this statement of understanding about where his only place of refuge lies:

> Though the fig tree does not bud
>   and there are no grapes on the vines,
> though the olive crop fails
>   and the fields produce no food,
> though there are no sheep in the pen
>   and no cattle in the stalls,
> yet I will rejoice in the LORD,
>   I will be joyful in God my Savior.

Anger is a reaction; trust is a choice. Feel the anger but make the choice anyway. God is where you go, even when you're angry. God is where you go, even when you're angry with him.

Friendly Fire

Up to this point, I have been speaking to those of you who have been traumatized, abused, and oppressed. Bad things have happened to you through no fault of your own—through the harm of others or circumstance—often leaving you full of rage. There are far too many of you, and God grieves for each one. He wants you to trust him with your anger and your pain. He asks you to wait upon his justice.

However, now I'd like to talk to another group of women. I do this with some level of care for fear of being misunderstood. So, please examine my words carefully, to determine if I am now speaking to you. There are some women with a great deal of indignation, bitterness, and rage because of bad things that have happened in their lives. However, for this group of women, in truth, your actions and attitudes have often been major contributors to these bad things. Although you may protest that you have no part or are not to blame, this is not the truth. Your actions and attitudes have helped determine the outcome you now protest against.

If you continue to deny your own part in the bad things that happen to you, you will not change. If you do not change, the outcome will not change; bad things will continue to happen to you. I have often seen this pattern occur in the lives of women and their relationships, which you'll read more about in the next chapter. If your life is predicated on a series of bad decisions, how can you reasonably expect only good things to occur in your life? The choices you make help determine the outcome. This is not an unfair life; this is a life of consequence.

In Scripture, there are the concepts of reaping and sowing, which are agricultural terms. To sow means to set something in motion, like when a farmer scatters seed. This seed scattering sets in motion the growth of crops. To reap, then, means to gather up what was set in motion by the sowing. This concept has a much wider application, of course, than just seeds and crops. Galatians 6:7 says, "Do not be deceived: God cannot be mocked. A man reaps what he sows." In 2 Corinthians 9:6 is this admonition: "Remember this: Whoever sows sparingly will also reap sparingly; and whoever sows generously will also reap generously."

If you look at yourself and see only a harvest of bad things, it would be valuable for you to take a look at what kind of seeds you're sowing in your life. If the majority of your seeds are impregnated with the spores of anger, this will affect your harvest.

With God's help, you can begin the process of giving up that negative seed and replacing it with the seed that comes from God. This kind of seed produces the fruit of the Spirit talked about in Galatians 5:22: love, joy, peace, patience, kindness, goodness, faithfulness, gentleness, and self-control.

There are also some of you who believe life treats you unfairly because the standard of fairness you set for yourself is different from the standard you apply to others. You, in essence, elevate your own needs, wants, and desires to the top of every list. You have wholeheartedly embraced the concept that you are special and have determined the world and everyone in it must agree to your definition, or the world is unfair. This is the definition of self-centeredness. If you believe you are deserving of always having one more chance, one more break, one more exception made, one more excuse accepted, one more explanation received than you are willing to give to others, life will seem unfair.

To help illustrate where I'm going with this, I'd like you to read the following passage. It comes from a parable Jesus told about the owner of a vineyard who went out to hire workers to harvest his crop. Beginning at the start of the morning, the owner contracted with workers to labor in his vineyard for a certain wage. As the day wore on and additional workers were needed, the owner went back and contracted with more until the final worker was only in the fields for a single hour before the day was done.

Up to this point, it's not a very controversial story. However, things get a little more interesting when it comes time for the workers to receive their pay. Imagine the indignation and cries of "foul!" when the workers discovered they were all to receive the exact same wage. This didn't sit well with the workers who had been hired first: "'These men who were hired last worked only one hour,' they said, 'and you have made them equal to us who have borne the burden of the work and the heat of the day'" (Matt. 20:12).

The owner of the vineyard, according to Jesus, didn't see the situation in the same light. "But he answered one of them, 'Friend, I am not being unfair to you. Didn't you agree to work for a denarius? Take your pay and go. I want to give the man who was hired last the same as I gave you" (Matt. 20:13–14). The workers who were hired first felt they were being treated unfairly by the owner because they worked longer for the same pay. Scripture says, "The workers who were hired about the eleventh hour came and each received a denarius. So when those came who were hired first, they expected to receive more. But each one of them also received a denarius" (Matt. 20:9–10). The workers expected something that didn't happen, and so they became angry and grumbled that they were being treated unfairly. The workers expected justice from the owner. When they didn't get it, they were angry.

This is not an easy parable. Frankly, it's one that makes me squirm because I can really see the point of view of the workers hired first. After all, they put in a full day's work, laboring in the hot sun, while the workers hired last only had to labor an hour. And they both received the same wage? What's fair about that?

What's fair, indeed? When those hired first agreed to work, they did so with the understanding they would receive a denarius. How much did they receive at the end of the day? They received a denarius, exactly what was promised and what they agreed to. How is that unfair? The owner of the vineyard had every right to contract with the workers as he saw fit. The vineyard, the money, the hiring was all in the control of the owner.

If the workers didn't want to agree to the terms, they could have declined the offer of work.

Were the workers treated unfairly? In truth, they were not. They received what they had every right to expect. When their expectations and assumptions went awry, they became angry.

The workers hired first felt wronged by the owner of the vineyard, even after he did exactly what he said he would do. They expected an exception would be made for them, based on what they saw happening to the other workers. They were wrong but insisted upon feeling wronged. Feeling wronged, they became angry and "grumbled."

Their words in verse 12 reveal the source of their indignation: "you have made them equal to us." If you are a woman who is angry, who grumbles and consistently thinks life is unfair, I want you to examine why that is. It may be you are operating under false assumptions and unrealistic expectations. It may be you feel you should be treated differently than others. Perhaps you are angry that you are treated equally when you expect to be treated better. It may be because you feel you are getting a raw deal. It may be because you look at the situations of your life and decide they are "unfair" to you even when they're not.

I say all this not to make you feel guilty but to open up your eyes. There is enough tragedy, injustice, and unfairness in the world, more than enough to go around. With all of that, it is not helpful to manufacture it where it does not exist. As the workers were grumbling and complaining, they remained focused on their own narrow point of view. Trapped within their own exclusive field of vision, they forgot there was another party, another point of view to be considered—that of the owner. From the owner's point of view, it was generosity; it was his money to do with as he saw fit.

As I've said before, women can have a very strong worldview. It can be so strong it's hard to see past it to take in the point of view of others. However, once that other point of view is factored in, it can change the way you see the situation. When you can change the way you see the situation, you can change the way you see yourself in the situation. When life is less unfair, you feel less the victim. When you feel less victimized, it is easier to diffuse your anger and recognize your own part and your own power in the situation. What you have power over, you can change and affect.

In truth, you will have power over some of your circumstances and not over others. However, you always have power over your attitude and response to those circumstances. You have power over how you view any given situation. In some situations, you may simply need to turn your anger over to God and wait on his justice. In other situations, you may need to re-evaluate your point of view, even if it means giving up your anger.

Note to Self

Every time you are treated unfairly, it hurts. A part of you knows that isn't the way it's supposed to be. The pain can be deep and lasting. The anger and resentment at this unfair treatment is real. Each new instance of unfair treatment compounds the one before it, until the weight of injustice in your life threatens to weigh you down. The only way to get out from under that burden is to take a look at each one, examine it honestly, and put it in its proper context. First, I'd like you to think back over your life and pinpoint those times when the pain of unfair treatment was most intense. I want you to identify specific instances.

I Was Treated Unfairly When . . .

1.

2.

3.

4.

5.

Next, I want you to go back over your list. (You may have more or less than five, given your life experiences. If you find you have trouble identifying specific instances, start as far back as you can remember and work forward.) Whenever appropriate, I'd like you to identify specific people who are associated with your unfair treatment. Often, you can feel that life in general treats you unfairly, but often this unfair treatment is associated with a specific person. Whenever there is a person or people involved, write this down.

For each of the experiences you've written down, I'd like you to answer the following question:

- As I think back at what happened to me, was there anything I could have done to avoid or prevent it?

For those of you who were traumatized or abused, this is not an easy question. Don't necessarily accept the first answer that comes to mind. This could be defensiveness or denial talking. Be still for a while. Set your anger aside. Allow yourself to delve deeper and the truth to emerge out of your silence. The truth is there; it often just gets drowned out. If you say no, it means you must face the truth that you were truly powerless over what happened to you. This sense of powerlessness is frightening. If you say yes, you indict yourself for some of your own pain.

Whether you say yes or no, you must allow yourself to grieve for the pain you suffered.

Now, ask yourself the next question:

- Knowing what I know now, how will this knowledge affect my life and choices today?

Each circumstance can be redeemed through insight and wisdom gained. Holding on to anger does not allow you to move into the processing stage, where what you've experienced becomes integrated into your life as a lesson learned and a source of growth.

Then, answer this third question:

- How has holding on to anger about this experience helped or harmed me?

It is possible for you to answer both "helped" and "harmed" from the same experience. Anger is often an initial shield and protector in severe situations. Its efficacy, however, fades with time, the more removed you are from the event. In a search for honesty, don't downplay either the "help" or "harm" aspect of your anger. You can acknowledge the help while appreciating the harm, making it easier for you to ultimately release the anger.

Finish up with this question:

- Based on what I've learned about myself through this experience, how will I use this knowledge positively going forward?

As I said before, what you've experienced in your life can be integrated as a lesson learned and source of growth. What is past is past, but what you do with it today and tomorrow has yet to be written. Treat yourself fairly by gleaning the good God promises in Romans 8:28: "And we know that in all things God works for the good of those who love him, who have been called according to his purpose." Again, this doesn't say in some things but in all things, including bad things that God knows will happen. Yet, while bad things are at work in the world, God is also working for your good because he loves you.

Dear God, I confess to you that life has treated me unfairly. I confess my anger over this mistreatment and give it to you. Help me to trust you to provide justice where it is due. Help me to wait upon your timing for that justice, knowing it will happen even if I don't see it. I confess I have looked at the world through a lens of injustice and have missed blessings you meant for me to experience and take joy in. As I work through my anger, help me to turn over to you the things I cannot control and strengthen me to address the things I can change in my own heart and life. I call on the power of your Spirit to transform me and renew my mind. Help me to get rid of all my anger, bitterness, and rage, leaving room for the fruit of your Spirit to infuse my life, my heart, my soul.

7

Why Can't We All Just Get Along?

> What causes fights and quarrels among you? Don't they come from your desires that battle within you?
>
> James 4:1

As a woman, you place a high degree of importance on your relationships. If there are unresolved relationships in your life, they are a source of pain. Whether the pain is the acute sting of a recent relationship separation or the dull ache of an old wound, pain over time causes irritation, inflammation, and anger. Only through a process of personal closure to unresolved relationships can the wound heal and the pain be placed in perspective.

Connie glanced at the clock on the dresser, agitated by how late it was. Almost simultaneously she heard her husband call up to the bedroom from downstairs. Rob wanted to know when she'd be ready to leave, and it was obvious by his tone of voice he was irritated at her tardiness. He'd said to be ready at 5:30, and she still had six minutes left, according to the clock. "I'm coming," she yelled back, even as she pulled the dress over her head. She still had to finish her makeup and do something, anything, about her hair. Nothing was ever easy.

This party was for Rob's work. She didn't even really want to go, but it was expected. It was also expected that she would be on time. She tried, she really did, but things just kept getting in the way. Since gaining all that weight last fall, nothing she put on ever seemed to look right. Her face seemed immune to even the most expensive cosmetics, and her hair could never be counted on to turn out the same way from one day to the next. Unfortunately, this happened to be one of those "next" days. Rob would want her to look her best but didn't seem willing to give her the time to pull that off.

He called again from downstairs, and Connie felt a surge of anger. Why was he putting such pressure on her? What was the big deal if they were a few minutes late? As far as she was concerned, if they came late and left early, they were better off. She decided just to forget about it and hurriedly finished up. If being there on time was so important, then he'd just have to settle for what he got. This was as good as she was going to get, and if it wasn't good enough, that was his problem. As she snatched up her coat and purse and stomped downstairs, Rob was waiting. He looked like he wanted to say something but thought better of it as soon as he saw her expression. Connie barely looked at him as she strode through the front door. It was going to be a long ride to the party.

Inside the car, all was quiet. Rob thought about turning on the radio but decided against it. Instead, he concentrated on driving, bewildered at another of Connie's "moods." He never knew what triggered them because she refused to talk about them to him. He'd done or said something wrong, that was for sure. It was probably asking her a second time if she was ready to go. Yeah, that was probably it, but he was worried about getting there on time and traffic. With a quick dart of his eyes, he glanced over at Connie to see if a thaw had started. Nope, she stared straight ahead, with that look on her face, not saying a word.

On the outside, Connie was quiet, but on the inside she was carrying on a passionate, angry conversation with herself. Her inner thoughts were a jumble of indignation, still blaming Rob for the pressure to be ready on time, to "perform" for his work. Along with the anger was shame; Connie was ashamed to be so inadequate. She knew she didn't look as good as she should. She always felt less than others thought she should be. She never could, it seemed, break out of the prison of other people's expectations. Whenever she looked at herself through their eyes, she always came up short. It used to make her angry as a kid, and it hadn't gone away as an adult. She knew she didn't measure up, and that made her ashamed. At the same time, Connie hated being measured, and that made her mad. At this point, everything made her mad.

Intimate Relationships

It seems appropriate that so much anger should originate and propagate within the confines of the family. Family is the most intimate of relationships, and anger is an intimate expression.

Your pattern of anger is like an emotional fingerprint. It is unique to you. While there are cultural sources of communal frustrations, what has the power to make you really mad is deeply personal. It reveals who you are as a person; it showcases your sore spots and exposes your wounds. What makes you angry tells a great deal about who you are—not just who you are on the outside, but who you are on the inside. Anger exposes your personal story.

When you are angry, you reveal your feelings. You show the other person what causes you to be angry. When you give another person this knowledge, you give the other person power. Some of you do not want anyone to have this kind of power over you, so you hide your anger away where it cannot be seen. Hiding the anger conceals the source of your pain. Hiding the anger helps you feel safe.

Some of you do not want anyone to have this kind of power over you, so you conceal the real source of your pain through diversionary anger. Anger itself becomes a diversion, covering up the pain and insecurity of guilt, shame, and fear. When anger is displayed scattershot, it is difficult to follow the spread pattern back to the source. It has all the visceral satisfaction of anger unleashed while maintaining the secrecy of the source. Diversionary anger is a way of hiding in plain sight.

It is not unlike the military concept of countermeasures. When a missile or a torpedo is heading toward a target, the target becomes vulnerable. In order to divert and confuse the incoming threat, countermeasures, also called chaff, are deployed. The missile or the torpedo becomes confused as to the real target and is thrown off, where it explodes harmlessly (at least ideally) away from the real target. If people get too close to the pain that lies at the core of your anger, you may feel vulnerable and release the chaff of diversionary anger to avoid exposing the truth.

Resolution in Relationships

When a relationship is infested with hidden anger and unexposed truths, it is an unresolved relationship. Unresolved relationships, as I said before, are a source of pain. It is important to remember, however, that bringing resolution to a relationship does not mean the relationship will be good or positive or perfect. Bringing resolution to a relationship often means bringing clarity to that relationship. If the relationship is a hurtful or abusive one, bringing it into clearer focus will only make the reality of that truth more apparent. Resolving relationships does not whitewash them, it reveals them for what they are. When relationships are revealed for what they are, sometimes you must acknowledge difficult and hurtful truths. When relationships are revealed for what they are, they can finally be addressed.

Unresolved relationships cause pain. Pain produces anger. Anger keeps relationships unresolved. It would seem logical, then, that the way to deal with this cyclical equation would be to deal with the pain in order to resolve the relationship. This is where fear once again plays a pivotal role. You may be fearful of addressing the true source of your pain, especially if the source of your pain comes from deep within your family experience growing up.

Katie came to work with me originally because of depression and an eating disorder. Her mother was concerned because, at twenty-three, Katie was obese. She had a good job but was plagued by high absenteeism that threatened her employment. When she was at work, she was meticulous and thorough. But there were just too many days when she couldn't seem to make it in. Her weight never seemed to go down. It would plateau for a time, but then Katie would have a "down time" and up it would creep. Her mother wanted Katie "fixed" so she could be happy, attractive, and able to enter into a dating relationship, which somehow had eluded her during all of her high school and most of her college years. These were things Katie wanted also. She thought if she was more self-disciplined and went on a diet, this long-awaited relationship was sure to follow. What Katie came to realize was she couldn't have a healthy new relationship until she worked through some old, unresolved ones.

When Katie was eight, her parents divorced. At the time, Katie was both devastated and relieved. She was devastated at the loss of her life as she knew it and relieved at an end to the yelling and fighting between her parents. Over and over again, her mother told her this was for the better. Her mother assured her they would all be much happier. Katie attempted to adjust as best she could, learning how to act when she visited her father and doing her best in school so he'd be proud.

The older she got, the more strained her relationship with her father became. He remarried and started another family. It was more difficult to go over to visit because Katie and her sister no longer had him to themselves. They became just another kid in the home, except they weren't really like the other kids who actually lived there. It didn't seem right to her that she spent less time with him than his stepdaughters did.

In middle school, it got even worse. Katie began to make excuses for why she didn't want to go see him. Her mother completely took her side and intervened on her behalf. As much as she thought she really didn't want to see him, it devastated her once again to realize he didn't try very hard to change her mind.

From that point on, her relationship with him faded out to obligation and form. There were obligatory holiday get-togethers and cards around her birthday, but that was about it. Katie moved on with her life—or so she thought. Inside, she was furious at being abandoned so quickly, so effortlessly by someone she'd once loved with all her heart. She thought he had loved her but decided his love was mainly one of convenience. When it was convenient for him to love her and have a relationship with her, he did. When it became more difficult, he jettisoned her like so much excess baggage. That's how Katie came to feel about herself—excess baggage. If she was "convenient," she was lovable.

Stung by this view of herself, Katie turned to something else convenient to love; she turned to food. With food, she found a relationship she could control. Food was always there, always satisfying—at least for the moment. Whenever she felt fearful or stressed or inadequate or angry, she could always eat to feel better.

She hadn't worried about it much while still in school because the sheer busyness and activity level of college kept a lid on her weight. As soon as Katie graduated and got a job, however, things started to unravel. Even though she wanted to lose weight, she couldn't seem to. The heavier she got, the worse she felt. Her weight became just another manifestation of her view of herself as "excess baggage." The more out of control her life and her eating became, the angrier she got. The angrier she got, the more despair she felt. The more despair she felt, the deeper her depression. The more depressed she became, the harder it was to go to work and the easier it was to eat.

Katie dreamed of a new relationship but really had unresolved relationships to deal with first. She had to deal with the unresolved relationship with her father. Until she did this, she had an unresolved relationship with herself. Living within this fuzzy, unfocused, unresolved world was disconcerting, and in her discomfort Katie turned to food. In her despair, she stuffed her anger.

It took a great deal of courage for Katie to unpack her excess baggage. She had to open herself up to the pain of rejection and abandonment. She needed to go back and relive that horrible time in her life through the eyes of a young adult. She had to allow herself to grieve and mourn her loss, to be angry, without the familiar comfort of her old coping strategies. Once again, she needed to be vulnerable and experience the pain so she could move past it.

One of the hardest things Katie had to do was acknowledge the role her mother played in her pain. Up to this point, she had found solace in the camaraderie between herself and her mother. She was content to assign all the blame to her father and none to her mother. As she worked through her anger at her father, she discovered a deep well of resentment at her mother, kept locked away and hidden for years. Though her issues were painful and unsettling, Katie determined to get to the bottom of them and seek resolution. Hiding the pain and the anger was wreaking havoc in her life, just as she was on the cusp of really living it for herself. Anger at others and shame at herself resolved into determination to change and move forward. As clarity came to her feelings about her parents, Katie was able to see herself more clearly. She learned who she really was and what she needed to do.

Katie's story is not unique. It finds expression in most of the women I work with. If you have an unresolved relationship in your past, and it stays unresolved, it will cause your relationship with yourself to remain unfocused. When your relationship with yourself is unfocused, it will adversely affect every other relationship you have or will have.

The Battle Within

The verse that started this chapter is James 4:1: "What causes fights and quarrels among you? Don't they come from your desires that battle within you?" When relationships are unresolved, they lead to unfulfilled desires. These unfulfilled desires are constantly agitating within you, battling your best efforts at personal peace, contentment, and happiness. This battle leaves you weary and wary, angry and frustrated, which leads you to fight and quarrel against yourself and others. Quarreling leads to a breakdown in relationship. Quarrels are often a red flag, pointing to diversionary anger.

The book of Proverbs has a good deal to say on the subject of quarrels. I'd like you to read through the following verses, just to get a sense of the damage quarrelling does:

- Proverbs 13:10—"Pride only breeds quarrels, but wisdom is found in those who take advice."
- Proverbs 15:18—"A hot-tempered man stirs up dissension, but a patient man calms a quarrel."
- Proverbs 17:14—"Starting a quarrel is like breaching a dam; so drop the matter before a dispute breaks out."
- Proverbs 17:19—"He who loves a quarrel loves sin; he who builds a high gate invites destruction."
- Proverbs 19:13—"A foolish son is his father's ruin, and a quarrelsome wife is like a constant dripping."
- Proverbs 20:3—"It is to a man's honor to avoid strife, but every fool is quick to quarrel."
- Proverbs 21:9—"Better to live on a corner of the roof than share a house with a quarrelsome wife."
- Proverbs 22:10—"Drive out the mocker, and out goes strife; quarrels and insults are ended."

- Proverbs 25:24—"Better to live on the corner of the roof than share a house with a quarrelsome wife."
- Proverbs 26:17—"Like one who seizes a dog by the ears is a passer-by who meddles in a quarrel not his own."
- Proverbs 26:20—"Without wood a fire goes out; without gossip a quarrel dies down."
- Proverbs 26:21—"As coal to embers and as wood to fire, so is a quarrelsome man for kindling strife."
- Proverbs 27:15—"A quarrelsome wife is like a constant dripping on a rainy day."

Undoubtedly, you picked up the theme specific to women. It is no coincidence that the admonition against this kind of quarrelsome behavior has its backdrop in a woman's relationships. Twice (19:13; 27:15) a quarrelsome wife is compared to a constant dripping and twice (21:9; 25:24) a woman's quarrelsome attitude is shown to drive family members away. Because women put such high value on relationships, it is tragic how many become so disagreeable, angry, and quarrelsome that they end up driving away the people they love most in life—their families.

The Bible clearly points to the problems inherent in a pattern of being quarrelsome. You've seen the passages specific to women, but I think there is something for women to gain out of examining the others.

Proverbs 13:10—"Pride only breeds quarrels, but wisdom is found in those who take advice." If you have been hurt by unmet needs and unfulfilled desires, you may have a tendency to concentrate exclusively on your own pain and position. In the last chapter, you read about the concept of victimhood. Wearing this mantle can turn into a source of identity and a source of perverse pride. This pride may interfere with your willingness to listen to others, take advice, and alter your perceptions. This is especially true if the advice is to let go of your anger so you can repair and clarify unresolved relationships.

Proverbs 15:18—"A hot-tempered man stirs up dissension, but a patient man calms a quarrel." Anger can produce a state of heightened anxiety and watchfulness. Anger can distort events and twist them into unintended shapes. Anger keeps you hot-tempered and itching for a fight, so much so that your attitude actually stirs up dissension. Being patient, however, is said to calm a quarrel. When you are able to turn your anger over to God, you are able to patiently wait for him to exact justice for you. Being patient keeps you calm and better able to realistically assess a given situation. Being calm leaves room for grace.

Proverbs 17:14—"Starting a quarrel is like breaching a dam; so drop the matter before a dispute breaks out." Nowhere is this truer, I think, than in working with couples. If both people have unresolved relationships, starting a quarrel between them unleashes a torrent of hidden issues. At times, my office has been flooded with accusations, recriminations, dire pronouncements, and tearful arguments. So many that it is difficult for the strength of the relationship to contain them all. That is why one of the skills I teach couples is how to "fight" fairly, passionately but also compassionately, truthfully but also gracefully. A knock-down-drag-out argument is simply not the most effective format for conflict resolution; instead it is a recipe for conflict conflagration.

Proverbs 17:19—"He who loves a quarrel loves sin; he who builds a high gate invites destruction." There are women I know, probably women you know, who love a good argument. It seems they like nothing better than to fight about nearly everything. If you are one of these women, you know deep down how much satisfaction you get out of unleashing your temper. I want you to hear something: even if the source of your anger comes from sin committed against you, that does not absolve you from responsibility in how you conduct yourself and express your anger. If that were the case, then an abuser who was abused would be free from guilt. If that were true, no one could be held responsible for their own wrongful actions because everyone has been wronged by someone. In order to heal and get over your anger, you need to start seeing it in its proper context—as a high gate you've built for protection. As this verse cautions, though a high gate does provide protection, it also invites destruction. If you doubt that, just think about the effect your anger has on those you love. Ask yourself—is your anger protecting or destroying your family relationships?

Proverbs 20:3— "*It is to a man's honor to avoid strife, but every fool is quick to quarrel.*" This is not the "doormat" proverb. It does not say that you should go about your life keeping your mouth shut in order to avoid problems. Rather, this verse cautions you to avoid strife. Strife is defined as a "bitter sometimes violent conflict or dissention" and as an "exertion or contention for superiority." Strife is quarrel fueled by anger and hostility. As such, it will not produce the desired results of resolution. Instead, it fans the flames of conflict. It is to your credit to avoid it and find another way to get your needs met.

Proverbs 22:10—"*Drive out the mocker, and out goes strife; quarrels and insults are ended.*" Did you know that you have a "mocker" inside your head? This is that negative voice you've read about that puts you down and devalues you. This voice is fueled by all the false, destructive, and unkind things said against you and things done to you. When this voice says you are not lovable, it mocks the truth of God's love for you. For you to get over your anger and begin to have an authentic, healthy relationship with yourself, you must drive this mocker out. When you do, out goes strife, internal quarrels, and self-inflicted insults. You declare peace with yourself and gain the clarity you need to resolve other relationships in your life.

Proverbs 26:17—"*Like one who seizes a dog by the ears is a passer-by who meddles in a quarrel not his own.*" Every one of you has been damaged by sin in your life—your own sin and the sins perpetrated against you. You are a casualty of a war raging. This war takes place in your life but also in realms beyond your comprehension. Ephesians 6:12 puts it this way: "For our struggle is not against flesh and blood, but against the rulers, against the authorities, against the powers of this dark world and against the spiritual forces of evil in the heavenly realms." There have been times, listening to stories of horrific abuse and trauma, I have a clearer picture of what this verse speaks to. What I want you to take from this verse is to be careful about entering into quarrels; you may not be aware of the forces arrayed against you. If you have wandered into a battle of this kind, remember that the battle belongs to the Lord. He has and always will fight for you.

Proverbs 26:20—"*Without wood a fire goes out; without gossip a quarrel dies down.*" Become aware of what sort of fuel incites your anger. Learn to be discerning. Refrain from indignation and umbrage at unsubstantiated rumors and gossip. Not only is this sort of behavior destructive, it often diverts you from your own work of reflection and recovery. Gossip is called a "choice morsel" in Proverbs 18:8 and 26:22. Don't let it tempt you and veer you away from doing your own work.

Proverbs 26:21—"*As coal to embers and as wood to fire, so is a quarrelsome man for kindling strife.*" It is helpful to know you are not the only hurt person in the world. Others are also hurt and carry the scars of their pain. In other words, there is an overabundance of fuel in this world to fan the flames of anger within relationships. An old saying is that it takes two to tango. If you insist on being a quarrelsome person, you will find a willing partner; you are sure to find plenty of opportunity to kindle strife.

If you have developed the strategy of being combative with others, I urge you to reconsider how effective this is in meeting your needs and filling the desires of your heart. This attitude forces a wedge between you and others. It destroys the very relationships you seek to create, maintain, and strengthen. It sours your mind and warps your viewpoint. It turns the world into a battleground, an adversarial exercise that must be waged day after day. It leaves you no room for peace. When, in your anger, people become your enemy, all your relationships will remain tainted and unresolved.

Rewriting History

There is another way a relationship can remain unresolved. This is when the same relationship is played out over and over, just with different people. Repetition is substituted for resolution. This relationship redo seeks to bring resolution to a previous relationship but rarely accomplishes this purpose. Sadly, it often results in additional pain and heartache. As the pain piles up, so does the anger. As disappointment after disappointment is realized, hope is crushed. As compelling and understandable as this strategy is, it is not possible to right a wrong by proxy.

Relationships are very precious to God. He is the beneficiary of the very first relationship. In Genesis 1:26, God uses the phrase "Let us make man in our image." God is not singular, he is plural. Before you or I entered the scene, he existed in relationship. Once he created man, in Genesis 2:18 God said, "It is not good for the man to be alone." He wanted people to be in relationship with each other. God is in relationship and values relationship. Relationship is so important, he sacrificed his only Son to heal the relationship with mankind broken by sin (2 Cor. 5:18).

If God so values relationships, so should you; you should not enter into one lightly. Nor should you enter into one in hopes of rewriting another. I have often seen this happen. A woman with a poor relationship with her father will enter into a relationship with a man very like him, in hopes of a different outcome. She may sacrifice her personality, her hopes, her dreams, even her virginity in exchange for the love she did not receive. She may marry a judgmental, rigid man in hopes of gaining the approval and acceptance withheld in the past. Because her relationship with her father is still unresolved, her relationship with herself is unresolved, and this irresolution will extend into any current relationship.

You also should not enter into a relationship expecting your current relationship to right the wrongs of the past. If you have an unresolved relationship causing you pain, you may be tempted to place all your expectations for relief in a current relationship. You may feel a sense of entitlement within this new relationship because of the pain you feel from old, unresolved ones. You may become angry when your current relationship fails to live up to this expectation and begin to shift blame from your past relationship to your present one. Thus blindsided by an unrealistic and unfair expectation, the person you are in a current relationship with may respond back in anger, starting a cycle of resentment.

Jesus said in Matthew 6:34, "Each day has enough trouble of its own." From what I've learned in my years of counseling, I can state that in the same way each relationship has enough trouble of its own! Relationships need to stand on their own. Each person you enter into relationship with needs the freedom to be who they are, not a reflection of someone else or as a projection of someone you want them to be. That is not the truth. Healthy relationships are based on truth.

Note to Self

For this section, I'd like you to take the time to really think about and evaluate the significant relationships in your life. These may be with parents, spouses, siblings, children, mentors, or extended family. You don't have to justify why a relationship is significant to you. I'd like you to include your relationship to God, whether or not you feel you're where you should be spiritually. I recognize this could be a long list.

As you think about significant relationships, I'd like you to be aware of any strained or broken relationships you have. Even if you have not spoken to that person in years, the fact your relationship is broken *is* significant. Start with the relationship you have with yourself and end with the relationship you have with God. Fill in the middle with your other self-identified significant relationships.

For those of you with isolated lives and small families, you may not come up with ten. If not, just move up your relationship to God—but leave at least one spot open. I think you'll find that as you do this exercise, a hidden relationship will surface. Perhaps one you haven't thought of in years.

For those of you with large families, you're going to need another piece of paper! Don't try to shorten this exercise just because you have many relationships to put down. Your relationships are important, every one of them, and deserve a periodic review. Go ahead and write them down.

My Significant Relationships

1. With myself
2.
3.
4.
5.
6.
7.
8.
9.
10. With God

Because it is important to start with yourself, I'd like you to take the time to write down your personal story. This is the story of your heartache, your pain, your vulnerability. It's the story you normally try so hard to cover up and protect. Whatever caused or causes you pain, I want you to write it down. Start as far back as you can remember and move forward. Think about your life growing up, the highlights and the times of despair, humiliation, shame, or difficulty. Take it all the way up to the present.

Some of you may have done this before back at the end of chapter 4. However, I suspect many of you were not yet ready to take this step. For some of you, this will be difficult to do. You've spent a great deal of energy trying to forget this story. You've gotten so good at suppressing it, you may find you have trouble drawing it out now. In order to help draw it out, I'd like you to utilize pictures.

The first thing I'd like you to do is go to whatever box or collection you may have of any family picture or pictures from your life and go through them. Often, memories are awakened by looking at pictures. You remember a person, a house, a toy, a car, a childhood friend, a relative. All of these things can bring other memories to the surface.

The other way you can use pictures is to draw one. Initially, it may be difficult—even frightening—for you to think about putting your pain down in words. If this is a barrier for you, start first by interpreting your pain visually. Use crayons, colored pencils, markers, watercolor or even oil-based paint. If you have a preferred medium, go ahead and use it. You are seeking to connect with the source of your pain through a different avenue than the written word. Once you've identified the feelings, you can begin to articulate the source.

If you are a musician or relate to feelings through music, you may find you have success in composing a song or using parts of songs you've heard to express yourself. Others of you will need to express your story in an allegory or a poem. Instead of using colors to evoke feelings, you will use poetic or allegorical imagery.

Often, writing things down is difficult at first, so it is necessary to prime the pump, so to speak. So if no words come initially, don't give up. Be creative about ways to connect to your pain and your story. Once you've made connection, I am hopeful you will find that words flow more easily. And don't worry about spell-check or grammar, punctuation, or capital letters. This isn't an English assignment. Reject any barriers to connecting to your story. Don't be diverted by this sort of chaff; hone in on your target.

I'm going to leave a page in this book for you to write down your story. For some of you, this will be all the room you need. For many others, it doesn't even begin to provide you the needed space. In that case, create your story in the medium that suits you best and then use this page to write down the highlights. Or use this page as a marker, where you can place your own written story. The blank space is an invitation not to put this off or keep reading or convince yourself you don't really need to do this. You do. The effort you extend will be worth it.

My Personal Story

My Personal Story (cont.)

As you consider your story, I'd like you to think about the countermeasures you bring to bear when someone comes too close to the truth of your pain, to the truth of the guilt, shame, and fear you feel. Sometimes women will be quick to reveal their pain but hesitant to expose their fears. All of these need to be on the table. Your anger is a response to them all.

Your countermeasures are your chaff, your diversionary anger or behaviors you send up and out from your life in order to avoid dealing with the pain, guilt, shame, and fear. All of these countermeasures adversely affect your relationships. For many of them, you create a new relationship with the countermeasure and substitute it for a relationship with another person.

In order to get you started, here are just some countermeasures I've encountered in my years as a counselor:

- addictions
- alcoholism
- depression
- eating disorders
- frigidity
- gambling
- hypochondrias
- irresponsibility
- irritability
- judgmentalism
- lying
- overcommitment
- panic or anxiety
- perfectionism
- self-aggrandizement
- sexual promiscuity

- smoking
- substance abuse
- vicarious living
- workaholism

This is by no means an exhaustive list but is provided for you to use in order to stimulate an honest appraisal of your own attitudes and behaviors. Another way to identify problem behaviors is by asking the following questions:

- Have any family members or close friends ever spoken to you about a particular behavior they found troubling or that caused them concern?
- Have you ever encountered employment problems due to a pattern of behavior?
- Have you ever lost a relationship because of a certain behavior?
- Are there any behaviors you feel unable to control?

After thinking through these things, go ahead and write down the countermeasures you've identified.

My Countermeasures

1.
2.
3.
4.
5.

Now that you've identified your countermeasures, I want you to be alert to when they are triggered and ask yourself the following:

- What was happening to me at the time?
- What was I thinking about?
- Did I mean to react that way, or was I surprised by my reaction?
- How else could I have reacted?

My hope and prayer is you will begin to clearly identify the areas in your own life that need closure and healing. As you deal with these issues, it will free you to deal with your relationships unencumbered by the pain of the past. Some of these relationships will need to be reevaluated and refreshed. Others will need to be reevaluated and jettisoned. Some will need to be mourned and released. Others will need to be acknowledged and celebrated.

Go back to your list of significant relationships. Beside each one that you're able, write down either *rejoice, reevaluate, refresh, repair,* or *release.* This includes your relationship with yourself and with God. One of the wonderful things about relationships is their capacity for repair. Identify how you feel about each.

- For those you mark as "rejoice," do so! Hug, write, call, laugh, email, praise—actively celebrate that relationship.
- For those you mark as "reevaluate," take the time to do so. If you need to separate for a time, make appropriate plans. If you need help to reevaluate, seek out family, friends, a counselor, pastor, or therapist—whoever you feel would be most insightful. (If you want to use someone else on your list, make sure that person falls under the "rejoice" category.)
- For those you mark as "refresh," make the effort to reestablish contact with that person. If the relationship has gotten stale or neglected, commit to the time it will take

to truly bring refreshment. Recognize you may need to start slowly and rebuild trust, on both sides.

- For those you mark as "repair," begin the work of reconciliation and renewal. This may require some confession on your part as the first step. Give it a try and see where it goes.
- For those you mark as "release," give yourself the time necessary to mourn and let go. My suspicion is if this was a relationship you were eager to release, you would have already done so. Be aware that you may have long ago released the person but have held on to the anger and it is that anger you must let go of to truly release the relationship.

In Revelation 3:20, Jesus promises, "Here I am! I stand at the door and knock. If anyone hears my voice and opens the door, I will come in and eat with him, and he with me." God, the originator and author of relationships, stands ready at all times to renew, refresh, and revive your relationship with him. His love and truth can revitalize your relationship with yourself and guide your relationships with others.

You stand at the door to my heart and knock. You stand at the door to my anger and ask to be allowed inside. I confess I've been ashamed for you to see what lies inside that door. I confess I have wanted to keep what lies inside that door to myself. I confess to you, Father, this anger is poisoning my relationships. Anger has become an idol in my life that I have worshiped and turned to for solace. Free me from my anger, almighty God. Release me from its chains. Drive out the mocker from inside my head. Help me to hear only your voice, as you sing over me with love and grace.

$$\equiv 8 \equiv$$

Can I Have a Truce
with My Body?

Rachel said to her father, "Don't be angry, my lord, that I cannot
stand up in your presence; I'm having my period."

Genesis 31:35

No discussion of women's anger would be complete without
acknowledging the physical and hormonal influences over the
course of your life—from puberty to post-menopause. Each
stage has its own challenges. Whatever the phase, there are some
basic commonsense steps you can take to treat your body gently.
I have found that women in their anger can harbor a great deal
of animosity toward their bodies.

Every month, Sherry felt attacked by her own body. The
truce never lasted long, and before she knew it, she was back to
blowing up like a balloon with water weight, breaking out with

pimples, craving food like she was starving one minute and sick with a headache the next. Her front hurt, her back hurt, and even though she was so tired she could barely drag herself out of bed, sleep during this time was elusive.

If sleep was elusive, peace of mind was nonexistent. Everything bothered her. On a scale of one to ten, her irritation was constantly red-lining toward ten. When she wasn't angry, she was anxious, going through life with a knot in her stomach, sure disaster was about to occur but with no idea of where or why or exactly when. In this heightened state, nothing kept to its normal shape, from her body to her problems. Difficulties got fast-forwarded to despair, hardships to hopeless.

Since everything and everyone made her mad or sad, Sherry felt she was doing the world a favor by spending as little time in it as possible. At work, she did the best she could while swirling in a miasma of discomfort. At home, she vanished to her room along with most of the "good" snacks from the cabinet. Her family walked softly, kept their heads down, and waited for the storm to pass.

The Times of Your Life

Your life is shaped by your menstrual cycle. For some of you, your period runs in the background; you accommodate it but it does not control you. For others, the time leading up to and including your period is one of dread and discomfort. It's as if half the time you're yourself and the other half you turn into someone else, someone even you aren't that fond of.

This period-person often displays anger, irritation, defensiveness, and tears in greater measure than the non-period you. Irritations that dissipate or simmer under the surface during your normal days erupt to the surface during your period. Anxieties and fears kept in check break out afresh in despair.

I'm not sure who coined the phrase "that time of the month," but it has come to have a pretty universal meaning in the lives of women and those around them. There are certain physical and emotional challenges you face before and during your period. Over the years, I've heard a litany of these complaints and observed several firsthand. Following is a list from information I found on WebMD:

- acne
- bloating
- tender breasts
- food cravings
- lack of energy
- cramps
- headaches
- low back pain
- sadness, anger, anxiety
- less alert
- trouble focusing
- isolation from family and friends
- acting with hostility or forcefulness

That's quite a bit to deal with. All of this is influenced by the interplay of hormones. When you menstruate, your estrogen and progesterone levels drop. When you ovulate, your estrogen and progesterone levels rise. Up and down, up and down, every month—or, if you are an average woman, every twenty-eight days. Most of you are intimately aware of the effects of that fluctuation in estrogen and progesterone that occur during menstruation even if you don't always understand the physical mechanisms involved.

Women have a lot to deal with during "that time of the month." But if that weren't enough, now there's information about the *other* time of the month, not during menstruation but during ovulation, when estrogen and progesterone levels rise about halfway through the menstrual cycle. During this time, you may be more susceptible to the following:

- migraines
- asthma or arthritis
- dental issues with increased sensitivity to plaque and gingivitis
- acne
- sluggishness

These symptoms are what can occur during normal menstrual cycles. Because each woman is different, your experiences will be different in specifics, but probably you found some level of commonality in the overall effects. These effects continue as long as you maintain a regular menstrual cycle.

As you age, you will enter a physical phase known as perimenopause. This is when your ovaries begin to decrease their production of estrogen, generally when you are in your forties. This phase can last up to several years and ends a year after your last period, when you become postmenopausal. Also from WebMD, here are what women often experience during perimenopause and menopause.

Perimenopause:

- hot flashes
- breast tenderness
- worsening of premenstrual symptoms

- decreased libido
- fatigue
- irregular periods
- vaginal dryness
- urine leakage or urgency
- mood swings
- difficulty sleeping

Menopause:

- irregular or skipped periods
- insomnia
- mood swings
- fatigue
- depression
- irritability
- racing heart
- headaches
- joint and muscle aches and pains
- changes in libido
- vaginal dryness
- bladder control problems

Taken together, these are some lists! I have heard the frustration, irritation, weariness, and anger of women over a life affected by these symptoms. Frankly, it's not surprising to me that some women should be so adversely affected by them; what's surprising to me is that more women aren't adversely affected by them. As women, you are often able to take these effects in stride and get on with your lives. You don't talk about it, you don't broadcast it; you just deal with it and do the best you can.

That heartens me but also concerns me because this can be just one more thing women have been asked to keep quiet about, to hide from view. Many women who were taught to stuff their anger were also taught not to discuss anything having to do with "female issues." It's as if they were made to feel dirty for having their period and had to keep quiet about it. Many Christian women have internalized the biblical term "unclean" when it comes to the menstrual cycle, as presented in Leviticus 15. This can lead to feelings of shame. That shame is then stuffed right alongside those negative feelings of guilt, fear, oppression, injustice, and pain—the sources of your anger. This ties your anger even more tightly to your periods. Many women who feel compelled to keep a lid on their anger generally find a ready-made avenue for venting during "that time of the month."

The Author of Your Period

If your period has become a cyclical ordeal, tied through anger to shame, frustration, and pain, you may very well be angry at God. After all, as the Creator of all things, he is the author of your period. So, in your eyes, this may be his fault and you're not too happy about it. He's the one who declared you "unclean" in the first place, and all of this seems so unfair. He didn't design men with this complex hormonal interplay. This may be one more way you feel disadvantaged by being female. You can understand the world's prejudice and oppression but may wonder why God set his creation up this way.

I'm not a doctor or a biblical scholar so I tend to look at this issue from a little different vantage point. I'm a therapist who seeks to understand the nature of people and why they do certain things. Reading over these lists, I think it can be easy to interpret these symptoms as a female disadvantage. But that doesn't make sense to me, knowing what I know about a loving God. Rather than highlight some sort of menstrual disadvantage, if I hold this situation up to the template of what I know about God's nature and why he does certain things, a different picture emerges.

The things God has made are good (Gen. 1:31). Since God created the female reproductive system, it is a good thing. There are few things more amazingly complex and beautiful than the process through which new life is created, nurtured, and protected. The menstrual cycle itself is a physical reminder of a spiritual truth: God's promise of rebirth and renewal.

God designed your body with an eye to unity (1 Cor. 12:22–25). There is nothing shameful about the female reproductive system. Listen to this passage, thinking about how you view your own body.

> On the contrary, those parts of the body that seem to be weaker are indispensable, and the parts that we think are less honorable we treat with special honor. And the parts that are unpresentable are treated with special modesty, while our presentable parts need no special treatment. But God has combined the members of the body and has given greater honor to the parts that lacked it, so that there should be no division in the body, but that its parts should have equal concern for each other.

Your body is specially designed so that all parts are honored, in concern and unity.

God is not a God of disorder but of peace (1 Cor. 14:33). From the lists of symptoms given throughout this chapter, it can appear that as soon as a young girl enters into puberty, her life is tossed back and forth on the pitching seas of monthly hormonal change.

This could be viewed as a life of disorder, but God is not a God of disorder but of peace. Therefore, with God's help, it is possible to maintain your emotional stability amid physical fluctuations.

God thinks you are beautiful (1 Peter 3:4). Unlike the world, who expects you to hide what you are, including your anger and your period, God knows everything about you and thinks you are beautiful. Through his Spirit, he gives you the ability to live in quiet, not chaos, and in gentleness, not hostility, at all times. There is no caveat here about only during certain times of the month.

God is able to help you achieve self-control (Gal. 5:23). This self-control is a vital fruit of the Spirit for you to have as a woman, given that your hormonal cycle will affect your mood. Many women express despair at how out of control they can become during their period. This reminds me of Proverbs 25:28, which says when you find yourself out of control, you are like a city whose walls are broken down. If you have erected walls to keep in your anger, they will tend to come tumbling down during this time.

The way you were made is not a reason to be angry at God. The way you were made is not an excuse to vent your anger. The way you were made is not a reason to be ashamed and stuff your anger. God gives you the promise of his love, the beauty of his creative energies, and the assurance of his Spirit. Your body is not your enemy, it is your ally at all times, but especially as you navigate your monthly cycles. You can live a self-controlled life every day of the month.

Positives for Your Period

No matter what phase of your menstrual cycle or phase of life, there are some basic things you can do to help you feel better.

Most of these aren't unique to women; they are universal for people in general.

- eat healthily
- maintain a healthy weight
- be careful what you put into your body
- exercise
- take a multivitamin
- stay hydrated
- get restful sleep
- consider hormonal support

Your body can be your partner in managing your monthly cycle. Over the course of my work, I've come to realize these steps are simple but not necessarily easy. For each one, you will probably have some barriers to overcome. Discovering and understanding what those barriers are is the first step in moving around them.

Eat Healthily

Eating healthily is all about the choices you make. Stay alert and in control and you'll make positive, healthy choices. Become distracted and eat on autopilot and you'll sabotage your health. When you don't feel well, it's easier to become discouraged and frustrated. When you feel sluggish and weighed down by what you eat, it's tempting to call on anger as a stimulant. You get angry at yourself for what you've eaten and you get angry at others to vent your frustration. Make healthy choices and there won't be any need for recriminations or regret.

Most women are aware of the need for healthy eating but find barriers along the pathway to better choices. One barrier to eating healthily is the plethora of processed foods available. These are foods that are already cooked, baked, fried, or put together for you. They include cookies, crackers, and all kinds of snack foods. They are quick and convenient. However, they can also be full of calories, fat, and sodium, as well as empty of nutrition. These types of foods are often what you turn to as comfort food to help manage feelings of anxiety, sadness, boredom, loneliness, and discomfort. They're also tempting to turn to during hormone-induced cravings. Comfort foods, in the long run, don't really provide you with anything because they leave you nutritionally deprived.

In order to eat healthily, you need to pay attention to those commercials you see on television and hear on the radio. Healthy eating simply includes consuming a variety of fruits and vegetables every day. These whole foods are packed with power—nutrients and fiber.

FOOD PYRAMID

In several of my books, I've encouraged people to go to the Department of Agriculture's website on healthy eating, found at mypyramid.gov. The food pyramid presented there has been updated since the first time I recommended it, and it's better than ever. Using the visual of the food pyramid is a way for you to track what a healthy diet looks like and provides insight into how to make healthy food choices:

- Starting from the left, the largest section represents the grains category, including breads, crackers, and cereals. Whenever possible, look for whole grains on the ingredient list of the foods you buy. These are grains that are used in their "whole" state, without being processed. During processing, dietary fiber and nutrients can be lost. Whole grains add more fiber to your system and take more time to digest, so you feel full longer.

- The next section represents vegetables, with a preference for dark green and orange vegetables. For vegetables, you want to think variety and quantity. You are also encouraged to eat more dry beans and peas.

- Then comes the slice of the pyramid representing fruits. You'll notice that this slice is a bit smaller than the green slice for vegetables. Fruits are wonderful for you but can also contain larger amounts of sugar. You are also reminded to avoid consuming large amounts of fruit juice, which can contain higher concentrations of sugar.

- The next slice in the pyramid is really a sliver not a slice, and it represents a category called oils. This is the fat category, with a preference for fats derived from fish, nuts, and vegetables. Solid fats like butter, margarine, lard, and shortening are to be used sparingly.

- The next wedge of the pyramid represents milk or dairy products. These should be low-fat or nonfat products whenever possible and include milk, yogurt, and various cheese products. For those of you who are lactose intolerant, there are lactose-free products available. This category is important because it's a source of needed calcium. Calcium is an important nutrient for women, especially in bone density and bone formation.

- The last section represents meats, beans, and protein foods, such as eggs. The preference here is toward lean protein sources that are baked, broiled, or grilled but not fried.

The pyramid also gives information on what it calls "discretionary calories" or those foods that add to the caloric intake represented by the pyramid, like increased fat content or sweets and sugars. Your daily caloric intake is compared to a budget, with the majority of your food budgeted for nutrition and the significantly smaller remainder for discretionary calories.

Over my years working with women and their eating issues, I have often found their eating habits to be flipped. The bulk of their caloric intake is devoted to foods from the discretionary calorie list, and then if they're still hungry or it's convenient or they're feeling guilty, they'll turn to the rest of the pyramid and eat a few healthy choices. This is unbalanced eating. When food is no longer used for nutrition, it can become instead a companion, a comforter, or even a lover when the relationship with food becomes your primary source of pleasure in life. When this happens, food is no longer food but an idol in your life. Food is meant by God to fuel your body and provide you with the nutrients you need to function and feel good. Food was not meant to be an idol worshiped for its illusion of comfort and pleasure.

Maintain a Healthy Weight

It is important not only to eat healthy foods but to eat them in the proper proportion. As a unique individual, you have an amount of calories needed each day and a weight range that is healthy and right for you. I wholeheartedly encourage you to visit with your primary care physician or gynecologist, if you have not done so already, and determine what a healthy weight looks like for you. Different women have different body types and frames, so two women of the same height arrive at different healthy weights.

Many women are as cyclical with their weight as they are with their periods. They lose and gain the same ten to fifteen to twenty pounds over and over again. When the weight is off, they're happy. When the weight is on, they're miserable. Because of the nature of yo-yo dieting, the tendency over time is for the weight to come back on, stay on, and increase. As you work with your doctor to find your healthy weight, come up with a plan to not only achieve that weight but also maintain it over time.

Be Careful What You Put into Your Body

How you feel and the health of your body depends not only on what you eat but also on what else you put into your body. If you are a smoker, I urge you to quit. Pumping nicotine into your system and smoke into your lungs is not good for you. The evidence of the damage done, apart from the dangers of lung cancer, is compelling. Smoking is an age accelerant, as its toxicity contributes to a more rapid decline of the body and overall health. If you smoke, you need to stop. This is also a conversation for you to have with your physician.

Be aware of the preservatives, additives, and hormones used in the foods you eat and drinks you consume. Many women have sensitivities and allergic reactions to these substances. Whenever possible, choose organic-type produce and foods. There are medical tests you can take that can help identify if your body is experiencing an ongoing allergic reaction to foods and other substances. If you suspect you are allergic to a certain food, eliminate it from your diet for a period of time and track your symptoms. When your body is under constant assault because of a sensitivity or allergic response, it will affect how you feel.

Be aware of the amount of alcohol you consume. As a chemical dependency professional, as well as a licensed counselor, I've seen the harm alcohol causes. If you have a problem with alcohol, don't drink at all. If you don't have a problem with alcohol, make sure to drink moderately. Not only do you need to be aware of the alcohol you are consuming, you need to also be aware of the extra calories in that alcohol. The more you drink, the more you impact the amount of calories consumed each day.

Lastly, be aware of the type and quantity of the drugs you take. These include, of course, over-the-counter, prescription, and illicit drugs. If you are concerned about what you're taking and how much, consider having a chemical dependency assessment done. These assessments factor in both legal and illegal substances and evaluate your level of dependency and abuse. If you're worried or if family and friends have expressed their concern, if your use has interfered with your job or with social and family functions, I urge you to seek professional advice and assessment. Please be aware that use and misuse of drugs is one strategy women use to self-medicate their feelings of anger. Because the anger is suppressed and not dealt with, it doesn't go away. Because the anger doesn't go away, the need for self-medicating doesn't go away, and use can change to abuse.

Exercise

Some of you will see the word *exercise* and want to run away from even the thought of exercising! Often, the very same women who were taught to stuff their emotions and hide their female issues were also taught that exercise wasn't something most women did. It was meant for men and athletic-type women but certainly not for them. Nothing could be farther from the truth. Exercise and the way your body responds to it is a gift from God to every woman.

Here are just a few benefits of exercise:

- increased flexibility
- stronger muscles
- increased bone density
- increased stamina and endurance
- lower risk of coronary artery disease
- lower blood pressure
- rise in good cholesterol levels and lower bad cholesterol levels
- help to control blood lipid abnormalities (that's from the American Heart Association)
- help to control diabetes
- help to control obesity
- increase survival rates for those who have suffered a heart attack
- improved feelings of depression
- improved quality of life
- relief from stress
- aid in sleep
- increased metabolism
- strengthening of the immune system
- relief from PMS symptoms
- positive benefits even with moderate changes in exercise level

This list is meant as an encouragement. It is meant to encourage those who already are engaged in regular exercise. Keep at it! It is meant to encourage those who have tried in the past but failed. Try again! It is meant to encourage those who have never exercised before. Give it a try!

If you fall into the latter category, make sure to see your doctor before you start an exercise program. To give yourself the best chance for success and decrease the potential for injury, work with a medical professional to help determine what the appropriate level of activity is for you right now. As your physical condition improves, your activity level can increase. Be intentional and thoughtful about your exercise. Maintaining a healthy weight is tremendously enhanced by adding exercise to your life.

Be creative in your exercise. It isn't just bench-pressing three hundred pounds or running a marathon. One of the best forms of exercise is walking. Make sure you have good, supportive shoes and are walking in a safe environment. You can also add more steps to your day by parking your car farther away from your destination and walking. You can take the stairs instead of the elevator or escalator or take a walk at lunch. There are plenty of helpful hints on the Department of Agriculture's website, as well as a way for you to track your exercise along with your food intake. With exercise, do whatever you can do. Do it consistently and do it cheerfully. Over time, you'll be amazed at what you're able to accomplish and how good you feel!

Take a Multivitamin

Even factoring in a healthy diet, researchers still realize it is not possible to get all of the vitamins and minerals you need each day. The way to remedy this deficiency is to take a nutritional supplement, like a multivitamin and mineral. You want to look for a supplement that allows for a high degree of bioavailability. This is a long word meaning the nutrients in the tablet or the pill or the powder can be easily absorbed into your system and utilized instead of passing through your system undigested and unused. Taking a multivitamin is fine, but you can't use what you don't digest, so make sure you buy the right kind.

God has designed your body to work at a microcellular level. Each nutrient, each vitamin, mineral, enzyme, and amino acid has a job to do. When all of the components are available to the body for use, the engine hums along smoothly. When vital nutrients are missing, problems, conditions, disease, and dysfunction occur.

If you are the type of person who doesn't like to take pills, find a powder or liquid form. If you have trouble remembering to take your vitamins, put the bottle or container next to your toothbrush in your bathroom or on your counter in the kitchen. Taking a multivitamin, just like eating healthy and exercising, is a habit you can adopt for yourself. Be diligent and thoughtful about it at first, and you'll find you're doing it as second nature in no time.

Stay Hydrated

Simply put, drink water. Sure, you can drink other liquids in moderation, but you need to consume the majority of your fluids each day in the form of water. If you don't have the benefit of good water out of your tap, buy a filtered water pitcher you can keep in your refrigerator. If you would rather not have all those plastic disposable water bottles clogging up the landfills, purchase a reusable water bottle. Water is an essential element of life and the body God gave you. You need enough water for your body to carry out its daily functions. One way for you to determine if you are fully hydrated is to check the color of your urine, if it is clear or a light yellow. (Be aware, however, that multivitamins will often affect urine color.) Another way is to track how often you go to the bathroom and the volume of urination. Your doctor can provide you with information and guidelines on the right amount of water for you.

I've always used the eight-by-eight rule as a good guideline—eight glasses of eight ounces each, for a total of sixty-four ounces per day. Again, this total is made up of all the liquids you drink, most of which should be water. It is possible, though rare, for a person to drink too much water. Again, your doctor is an excellent source of information on what is right for you.

Get Restful Sleep

One of the common complaints from women, especially those who are headed into menopause, is difficulty falling and staying asleep. If you have a problem with sleep, you may think there isn't anything you can do about it but just suffer. However, there are a variety of things you can do to work toward improving your sleep.

- *Keep to a regular sleep schedule.* Your release of hormones is tied to your wake and sleep patterns. As much as possible, stick to the same schedule, even on weekends. Your body will learn for itself when it's time to wake up and when it's time to sleep.
- *Prepare your sleep environment.*
  - ✓ Keep it dark.
  - ✓ Keep it quiet.
  - ✓ Keep it a comfortable temperature.
  - ✓ Sleep on a good quality, supportive mattress.
  - ✓ Have good air flow in the room.

- *Do not use tobacco or alcohol from the late afternoon on.* The nicotine in tobacco is a stimulant, and alcohol negatively affects your quality of sleep. Again, if you are a smoker or tobacco user, please take steps now to quit. If you drink in moderation, be aware of your nighttime consumption.
- *Keep your bedroom your bedroom.* Don't turn it into an auxiliary television room, computer room, or workstation. Your bedroom should be a place where you give your mind permission to rest, turn off, and go into "sleep" mode.
- *If you have trouble sleeping, try warm milk.* This may be an old remedy, but it really does have properties that can help you sleep. You can also use a small glass of decaffeinated hot tea. Make this more around four to six ounces than twelve to sixteen ounces or you'll end up waking during the night to use the bathroom!
- *Turn the clock around so you can't see it.* If you're having trouble sleeping, fixating on the changing time isn't exactly going to enhance your ability to relax and fall asleep.
- *Take a hot bath or shower just prior to going to bed.* Allowing your body to physically relax will assist your mind in triggering its internal shutoff switch.

Good sleep isn't an option for women—if you get it, great, if not, oh well. Poor sleep has been found to have greater negative health consequences for women than for men. A recent article from *Science News* highlighted research done by Duke University on the effects of poor sleep on men and women. In the past, much of the sleep research was done on men and was assumed to hold true for women. Not so, according to Edward Suarez, an associate professor at Duke University and the lead author of the study. "The study suggests that poor sleep—measured by the total amount of sleep, the degree of awakening during the night and, most importantly, how long it takes to get to sleep—may have more serious health consequences for women than for men. ... We found that for women, poor sleep is strongly associated with high levels of psychological distress, and greater feelings of hostility, depression and anger."[2] Your sleep is important to you physically and emotionally. It is a vital element of your overall well-being and health.

Consider Hormonal Support

If you suffer from extreme symptoms around your period, you don't have to suffer in silence. There is help available. Consider contacting your doctor to look into hormonal support. These can take a variety of forms, including homeopathic or naturopathic interventions as well as strictly pharmaceutical choices. Make sure you know what is being recommended and the side effects. Hormone replacement therapy (HRT) has a mixed track record, especially in the pharmaceutical arena. Whatever you choose—pharmaceutical, naturopathic, or homeopathic—make sure you understand it fully.

Again, your body can become your best friend when it comes to navigating successfully through your period. You don't have to become a prisoner to your symptoms and your moods. The better your health, the better you feel. The better you feel, the fewer barriers you will have to managing your period and your moods.

Note It and Come Back Later

I just want to mention one more thing on this topic of anger and "that time of the month." My wife, LaFon, is very wise. We were talking about this subject, and she said something profound that I wanted to pass along. She said she doesn't necessarily dismiss everything she gets angry about during her period as just a casualty of her hormones. Instead, she makes a note of what it is that made her angry, to think about later. She chooses not to indulge the anger right then because she recognizes it is not the best time for her to have an emotion-laden discussion. Instead, she notes it and comes back to it later, after her period is over and her emotions have settled.

Because women have a tendency to stuff hurts, you may neglect to recognize or resolve an issue that truly bothers you. However, during the emotional highs of your period, the issue can rise rapidly to the surface and escape from your carefully constructed containment. If you decide to give full vent to your anger at that moment, you may be in reaction mode and miss an opportunity for quiet reflection and consideration of the issue that has surfaced and bothers you. By waiting, you acknowledge the truth of the anger but also give yourself the time to examine it and determine the best course of action to resolve the issue. Waiting for the right moment isn't a defeat, it's a deferment. For highly emotional or volatile issues, timing can be the key to successful resolution.

I'm sure many of you have launched into a legitimate point with a loved one, only to realize your concerns have been downplayed or marginalized because of your emotional state. You may even have heard the question asked, "Are you having your period?" Sadly, this has too often been used as a way to avoid dealing with the truth of your concerns. By disconnecting your concern from your physiology, it may be easier for you to say what you need to say and for the other person to be in a better position to receive it.

Note to Self

It is time for you to be serious about your physical health so you can be better prepared to deal with your emotional health. I've always believed in the concept of "whole person," that you must deal with your issues from an emotional, relational, physical, and spiritual point of view, in order to enhance healing and recovery. How you feel physically has a tremendous influence over how you feel emotionally.

I would venture to guess that most of what you read in this chapter did not come as a complete surprise. Many of these things, as I said before, are common sense. What is uncommon and unique to each person is the set of personal barriers you must overcome to achieve your desire for better health. For some of you, those barriers come in the form of chronic conditions or even disease processes. For others, the barriers are psychological in nature. For most, there are always spiritual components to any barrier.

For this Note to Self section, I'd like you to go through and identify your personal barriers. Then I want you to come up with action steps you can take today to assist you in moving past those barriers.

Listed below are the components mentioned in this chapter. I'd like you to think about each one and write down any barrier you have to attaining that goal. Along with the barrier, write down a reason why. Naming the barrier isn't enough; you need to give a reason for why it exists.

If you have already achieved the goal as a regular pattern in your life, I'd like you to use the space to list why this aspect is so important to you. What are the benefits you derive from it and why are you motivated to continue?

Again, be honest with yourself and write down the truth you know. Don't give in to feeling guilty or ashamed about any of these goals. This isn't meant to show you where you've failed, it's meant to help you discover how to succeed.

1. Eat healthily

2. Maintain a healthy weight

3. Be careful what you put into your body

4. Exercise

5. Take a multivitamin

6. Stay hydrated

7. Get restful sleep

8. Consider hormonal support

Maybe you have a barrier to eating healthily because your food choices have always been a way to feed your emotions and not your body.

Maybe you have a barrier to maintaining a healthy weight because you have no idea what a healthy weight is for you.

Maybe you haven't been careful about what you put in your body because, to you, your body is the enemy and doesn't deserve to be taken care of and nurtured.

Maybe exercise conjures up a picture of a huffing, puffing, sweaty person who is vastly uncomfortable, and even the thought of doing anything strenuous is daunting.

Maybe you hate the thought of having to take a pill every day for the rest of your life and you really aren't convinced it isn't all some sort of scam to waste your money.

Maybe you don't want to drink water because you want to drink things like coffee or sodas during the day.

Maybe you've given up on ever really getting a good night's sleep because you've tried everything you can think of but nothing's worked.

Maybe you think you're just supposed to suffer through your menstrual symptoms, you and your immediate family, because you're worried about what the doctor might say or what you might have to do to make the situation better.

Maybe you wish your anger issues were just a matter of learning how to control your temper and say the right thing at the right time instead of making lifestyle changes and giving up behaviors you have always used and come to rely upon.

I'd like you to go through your list and circle the numbers where you have not been successful in achieving your goals. This is your barriers list, and it's a recitation of *why not*. When dealing with motivation, the *why nots* in your mind are often clambering incessantly to climb to the top of your consciousness. Some of them are legitimate issues that need to be factored into your life and actions. Others can be like whiny children, demanding your attention and validation. Only you know which are which.

Even if a barrier is legitimate, like a physical handicap or condition, I still want you to meditate on ways to mitigate the strength of that barrier. There are many people—society calls them heroes—who face significant challenges but refuse to quit in the face of them. Instead, with determination and courage, they press on to their goal, like Paul says in Philippians 3:12–14. More times than not, overcoming a barrier will require action; it will require *pressing on*. This presents a picture of moving forward even through opposition.

It is time for you to identify one way you can press on toward each of these goals in your life. I'm just looking for one. If you think of others, go ahead and put them down, but start with one. Start with one step toward the prize, and then when your foot is firmly planted going forward, move the other foot and take the next step. Step by step, press on to your goal.

Pressing On Past My Barriers

1. I Can Eat Healthily By . . .

2. I Can Maintain a Healthy Weight By . . .

3. I Can Be Careful What I Put into My Body By . . .

4. I Can Exercise By . . .

5. I Can Take a Multivitamin By . . .

6. I Can Stay Hydrated By . . .

7. I Can Get Restful Sleep By . . .

8. I Can Consider Hormonal Support By . . .

Please recognize that you are not required to take these steps alone. Whenever possible, engage the help and support of family and friends.

- Let your family know your goals and ask for their help in holding you accountable.
- Get together with a close and trusted friend, one who may have some of the same issues, and agree to partner together on your goals.
- Join a support group of like-minded people, all working toward the same goal.
- Ask for prayers of your church or faith community and be transparent about your challenges and victories.
- Meet with your doctor and partner together on your goals. If you don't have a primary care physician or gynecologist, ask around for referrals.
- Gain the help of a professional counselor or therapist if this chapter has uncovered or highlighted addiction issues that interfere with your health goals.
- Be intentional about any decisions regarding what to eat or what to drink. Make preparations to be successful. Remove

unwanted food or drink and purchase items more in line with your desires and goals.
- Act in accordance with what you want instead of just thinking about what you want.

More than anything, please realize you are not alone in this effort, because you are never alone. Your heavenly Father is aware of your struggles and your barriers. He understands your frustrations and the source of your anger. It is his desire for you to enjoy a healthy body, a healthy mind, and a healthy spirit.

Father, I thank you for making me a woman. I confess I haven't always felt this way and have, at times, been angry about it. I confess I have used this body you gave me and the phases you designed as an excuse to vent my anger to those around me. I ask for wisdom to recognize these phases and the strength to respond to myself and others with gentleness and self-control. Give me the courage to look at my behaviors and evaluate if I am helping or harming my overall health. My body is a temple of your Holy Spirit, O God. Help me to treat it accordingly, with praise and thanksgiving.

Part 3

Uprooting the Anger and Pruning the Branches

═══ 9 ═══

Learning the Power of Acceptance

Accept one another, then, just as Christ accepted you, in order to bring praise to God.

Romans 15:7

Many women live their whole lives trying to be someone they're not, trying desperately to hide who they are—or who they think they are. There is tremendous power in knowing who you are and accepting who you are. In the verse above, you can see that Christ has accepted you, and you are told to accept one another. You may have an easier time, however, accepting others than you do accepting yourself.

Sandra checked over her figures three times, but the answer was still the same. Inside, she felt that familiar feeling of dread

211

rise up from the bottom of her fear. She'd made a mistake. There was no other way to put it. And now she knew there was no other way to deal with it.

In the past, Sandra would have been in full panic mode by now. She would have looked for ways to pretend the mistake didn't exist. She would have devised an elaborate scaffold to camouflage and conceal the mistake. All the while, she would have lived in fear of discovery, terrified of her mistake and angry at herself for making it. Not anymore.

Calm down, Sandra, she told herself. *You're not expected to be perfect. What you are expected to do is report problems when you find them. The error is not your mistake; the error would be not to report it. It's all right. Just get up and do the right thing.*

Taking her worksheet with her, she went down the hall to her supervisor's office. *Just tell the truth,* she counseled herself as she knocked twice on the door. *It's going to be fine.*

Designed to Hold

Acceptance is an interesting word. It involves both the act of *accepting* as well as the fact of being *accepted*. In this way, it's kind of a two-way street. One of the corollary definitions of accepting is "to be able or designed to take hold, as in something added or applied, like a surface that will not accept ink." This is another two-way street. On the one hand is the surface and on the other hand is the ink. Acceptance happens when the first is primed to consent to the second.

I remember watching a master artisan create an ink drawing on fine linen paper. There was something spare yet elegant in the careful brushstrokes from which a blooming branch took shape. It was as if the paper itself was hungry to accept and drink in the ink that forever altered its surface. The artisan knew how much ink to put on the brush and how long to rest the brush on the paper, mindful of how much ink would be absorbed. The gentle precision was impressive and the drawing that resulted simply beautiful.

I think God is like that master artisan. The surface is your sense of self, and the ink is the truth of your life. Only when you learn to accept and drink in the truth will you become who God wants you to be. In order to accept yourself, to display the vital characteristic of self-acceptance, you must be able to take and hold the truth when it is applied to your life. As the definition says, I believe God has *designed* you to be able to do just that.

Many women, however, are not able to accept the truth. They are resistant to the truth and refuse to take it in. Truth, however, is persistent. It doesn't go away just because you want it to. Truth affects your life, whether you acknowledge it or not. Because you go to such lengths to shield yourself from the truth, its very persistence can be a source of frustration and anger. You just want the truth to give way to your preferred desire. When it doesn't, it can make you mad.

When you fight against the truth, you create a battle that doesn't need to take place. You use time, energy, and emotions that could be better used to accept and integrate it into your life. Because the truth is often painful, you believe you are shielding yourself from pain by denying, hiding, or reconstructing it. But the pain created by denying it outweighs the pain of accepting the truth. It is not unlike the way Scripture says discipline works: "No discipline seems pleasant at the time, but painful. Later on, however, it produces a harvest of righteousness and peace for those who have been trained by it" (Heb. 12:11). Accepting the truth, though painful, can produce a harvest of strength and resilience.

You need to ask yourself, *Am I willing to accept the truth?* This is a journey of discovery I've been privileged to help many women navigate. Often, they begin by admitting, no, they are not willing to accept the truth of their life, of themselves, of their past, of their families. Because they cannot accept the truth, they remain stuck in their pain and anger. Instead of accepting the truth, allowing it to alter them and move on, they prefer to remain where they are. They are under the illusion that it is better to maintain a clear, untouched canvas instead of risking what pattern will emerge in their lives when truth is absorbed. To them, the ink of truth does not produce a beautiful picture, it soils an illusion they've tried very hard to maintain. The surface of their denial rejects the ink of truth. When truth is attempted, it is not absorbed but repelled, resulting in an ugly, smeared mess.

The Perfect Denial

Perfectionism, as previously discussed, is not the truth. Perfectionism inhibits the surface of your life to accept the truth. This perfectionism can be applied to your entire life or just a sheltered part of it. As a Christian woman, you may have been brought up under the notion, either overtly presented or implied, that in order to be acceptable to God and to others you needed to be perfect or at least as close to perfect as you could possibly get. This is called "conditional love" and is a damaging form of emotional abuse. It can be couched in biblical clothing, but it hides a deception. Your desire for your life or some aspect of it to be "perfect" may appear to flood your life with meaning and purpose. Don't buy into this deception; just because something is pronounced as scriptural doesn't always mean it is. As 2 Corinthians 11:14 cautions, even Satan masquerades as an angel of light. Again, you must look at the nature of God and what you know of his character to interpret this concept of being worthy and being perfect.

In Matthew 5:48, in the middle of the Sermon on the Mount, Jesus says this: "Be perfect, therefore, as your heavenly Father is perfect." I believe many people misunderstand this verse because they overlook one word—*therefore*. This statement is a conclusion, based on all that Jesus has said up to this point. Jesus has been comparing what people normally do to God's standard for living, for acting and loving. Quite naturally, the standard people have comes woefully short. The conclusion, therefore, is to go with God's standard; to be perfect, as your heavenly Father is perfect.

This is God's standard, however, but it is not the threshold. It is the standard God wants you to live by, but it is not the threshold of his love. God does not wait until you are perfect before he loves you. Romans 5:8 speaks directly to this lie of perfectionism: "But God demonstrates his own love for us in this: While we were still sinners, Christ died for us." Or, put in a different way, "But God demonstrates his own love for you in this: Even though you're not perfect, Christ died for you." Love is the threshold; love is the motivation, not being perfect.

If you believe you must be perfect to be loved, this can be a source of unyielding anger. Deep down, you know it is impossible to be perfect. This is a reality borne out in Scripture, when

James says, "We all stumble in many ways" (James 3:2) or when John says, "If we claim to be without sin, we deceive ourselves and the truth is not in us" (1 John 1:8). Paul joins in when he says in Romans 3:23 that "all have sinned and fall short of the glory of God." Believing the lie of perfectionism can only lead to despair—if you can only be loved when you are perfect and it is impossible to be perfect, then you must conclude you are unlovable. Being thus punished for an impossibility screams of unfairness and injustice. It is the source of a great deal of anger in women who have often been subject to unfair standards, from personal conduct to physical attractiveness.

Perfectionism is also the source of a great deal of time, energy, and effort by women. I have known women who spent the better part of their lives trying desperately to live up to this image of perfection in order to feel worthy to be loved. In many cases, this deep desire and motivation are rooted in childhood and the withheld love and affection of a parent. It's almost as if a contract was signed between the daughter and the parent that read: if you are perfect, I will love you. If you are not perfect, I will not love you.

What you didn't realize as a child was the parent was not able to love in the first place and so set up this one-sided contract in order to justify his or her lack of love for you. The deficit was not on your part, it was on the part of an emotionally damaged parent.

This is ink many women repel. They do not want this truth absorbed into the surface of their lives because it will mar the desperately desired image they hold of that parent. They hold on to the "perfect" belief that if they can just be good enough, pretty enough, popular enough, successful enough, *enough* enough, the withheld love will be forthcoming. By making themselves responsible for this love, they believe they have control over it. But the continual disappointment and deep-down realization of the futility of their efforts only produces pain and anger. Sometimes in accepting a truth, you must give up a dream. Sometimes the truth that must be accepted is less than perfect.

The apostle Paul understood the pain of a less-than-perfect past. He started out his religious career searching for spiritual perfection, striving to become a Pharisee, an ultra-legalistic Jew. He speaks of the perfectionism he sought to attain as "confidence in the flesh" in Philippians 3:4. He goes on to list all of his claims to worthiness in the Jewish faith, concluding they were meaningless, especially when compared to the knowledge and understanding of God's grace in Christ. Paul tried his culture's definition of perfectionism and found it to be "rubbish." It didn't get him anywhere. Instead, his desire was to become like Christ.

I'd like you to read what he writes in Philippians 3:12–14, which was referenced in the last chapter:

> Not that I have already obtained all this, or have already been made perfect, but I press on to take hold of that for which Christ Jesus took hold of me. Brothers, I do not consider myself yet to have taken hold of it. But one thing I do: Forgetting what lies behind and straining toward what is ahead, I press on toward the goal to win the prize for which God has called me heavenward in Christ Jesus.

Paul is not stuck in a desire to be perfect anymore. He acknowledges in verse 12 that he is not perfect but doesn't allow that to slow him down. The rest of this passage clearly speaks about moving forward. Paul uses language like *press on* and *strain*.

Instead of beating himself up over the imperfections of the past or present, he chooses to accept this truth and move forward.

Paul accepts the truth of his own imperfection onto the surface of his life. He even goes one step further; he readily drinks in this imperfection. He doesn't try to hide it or conceal it; instead he puts it to use for God's glory. In 2 Corinthians 12, Paul struggles with what he calls a "thorn in the flesh." I don't know if anyone has come up with a definitive answer for what this was. Paul doesn't say, just that it was a "weakness." He asks God three times to remove it, but the answer comes back each time, no. Then Paul records this message he received from Christ and his conclusion from it: "But he said to me, 'My grace is sufficient for you, for my power is made perfect in weakness.' Therefore I will boast all the more gladly about my weaknesses, so that Christ's power may rest on me" (2 Cor. 12:9). Paul allows the truth of his weakness to absorb into and alter the surface of his life. He accepts it as a way for God to manifest his redemptive power. Rather than hide it, he reveals it so God's glory might also be revealed.

Dishonest Standards

When you use perfection as the standard by which you feel loved yourself or show love to others, this is a dishonest standard because it is impossible to attain. Leviticus 19:35 says, "Do not use dishonest standards when measuring length, weight or quantity" and Proverbs 11:1 says, "The LORD abhors dishonest scales, but accurate weights are his delight." If God abhors— or hates—dishonest scales when used on things like wheat or oil, how much more will he abhor dishonest scales when they are used against those he loves? Perfectionism is a dishonest standard used against you to withhold love and affection. Per-fectionism is a dishonest standard used by you to try to attain love and affection from others. Perfectionism is a dishonest standard used by you to withhold your love and affection from others. In any form, it must be jettisoned so that acceptance can do its work in your life.

This does not mean that you must give in to a substandard life. Rather, it means you must stop looking to yourself and others as the source of perfection. People are not perfect and will always disappoint. If you link your own happiness to always being treated fairly or to the other person always acting just as you want, you will be unhappy, because with people—including yourself—there is no *always*, there is only *sometimes*.

Yield yourself to God and allow him to strengthen you. This is the advice given in 2 Samuel 22:33: "It is God who arms me with strength and makes my way perfect." You are not able to achieve perfection on your own. However, God is able to make your way perfect. This is the essence of the promise given in Romans 8:28: "And we know that in all things God works for the good of those who love him, who have been called according to his purpose." This is the essence of God's redemptive power in your life and in the lives of others. He is able to factor the imperfect into his perfect plan and purposes. It's beyond me to understand how he does this. I just know that he does, because I've seen it in my own life and in the life of others.

Letting Go

Perfectionism can be a difficult mind-set to release because it can appear so *right*. Attempting to achieve perfection can feel so *righteous*, as Paul talks about in Philippians 3:9, speaking of his own quest. It can be tempting to forget the "therefore" and just seek to bring about the words of Jesus on your own: be perfect as your heavenly Father is perfect. There's just that problem of the "therefore." Because of your imperfection, your attempts to attain perfection on your own will always be imperfect.

Even the best attempts to be perfect will not succeed. One reason for this is because people mess up and aren't able to be perfect. Another reason is that people and God don't think alike. What you are absolutely sure is good and right and perfect may not be to God. Isaiah 55:8–9 says, "'For my thoughts are not your thoughts, neither are your ways my ways,' declares the LORD. 'As the heavens are higher than the earth, so are my ways higher than your ways and my thoughts than your thoughts.'" This is tragically brought home when working with women whose idea of perfection and righteousness have alienated their families, devastated their relationships, and compromised their health. Each was so sure what she was doing was right. Each was so sure what she was concealing needed to stay hidden. Each was so attached to the power of her anger she had trouble letting it go.

You may believe your anger is perfect; it may be the one thing you are absolutely sure about and, thus, unwilling to give up. This surety may allow you to feel justified in being angry and in determining how that anger is manifested in your life. But remember the caveat about your anger in James 1:19–20, where he says, "Everyone should be quick to listen, slow to speak and slow to become angry, for man's anger does not bring about the righteous life that God desires." Anger, no matter how right it feels, does not produce righteousness.

Set Free

Paula drove up and parked in front of the stucco building. It was raining outside, which only made the exterior appear drearier. Two large planters by the front entrance still held the remains of chrysanthemums and pansies from a summer now faded to fall. Just as she hesitated, fighting with herself over whether or not she really wanted to do this, the sliding glass doors were triggered. Their opening made up her mind, and she walked inside.

Her father's room, she found out from the woman at the reception desk, was on the second floor, to the right, past the sitting room. As she rode up the elevator, Paula reminded herself why she was here. Within the whirl of her emotions, she needed to be reminded.

Softly, she knocked on the door and went inside. He was waiting for her, sitting up in the chair. She allowed herself a small smile. Even at the end of his life, he was still true to form. It would have been completely out of character for him to allow her to see him lying in bed. The smile faltered as she realized how difficult it must have been for him to gather the energy to present himself this way. After all, he was dying.

She went over and kissed his cheek, pulling another chair over next to his. He told her in a thin voice that he was glad she'd come. He asked about her flight and how the kids were doing. A part of her responded automatically, just giving information. Another part of her was struggling with the conversation. There was so much more she wanted to say but knew she could not.

For several years, Paula had worked hard to put the bitterness and anger toward her father aside. Growing up, she had never felt any affection from him. His love for her seemed perfunctory and obligatory, just part of what he was expected to do, along with all the other "duties" in his life. After her parents divorced when Paula was in her early twenties, she found she didn't have much room for him in her life. He, in turn, made little effort to keep contact with her. They began a period of mutual estrangement, preferring no relationship to an awkward one.

Now in her fifties, she was the age her father was when he'd divorced. Divorced herself, she experienced an odd disconnect at the connection. This realization of commonality with someone she'd spent so many years disliking had been the first step in her journey to today.

There were so many things she wanted to say. She wanted to explain the work she'd done in her own life to come to grips with his emotional distance. She wanted to tell him she no longer held him responsible for his failure to live up to her expectations of what a father should be. She wanted to tell him she finally accepted him for who he was, instead of resenting him for not being who she wanted him to be. Looking at him, struggling to maintain even a conversation on travel and weather and grandchildren, Paula realized—once again—he was unable to handle her desires.

As she got up to leave, knowing it could be the last time she saw him, she gave herself one gift. Crouching down so their faces were at the same level, she held on to his hand, looked straight into his eyes, and said, "I love you, Dad," while she held his gaze.

Riding down in the elevator, searching in her purse for the tissues she'd brought, Paula allowed herself to believe he'd understood a little bit of all she meant by that statement. Whatever he was able to understand, she'd accept. Over the past year she'd done a lot of that—accept. She'd come to accept him, for who he was as a father, and she'd come to accept herself, for who she was with him as a father.

The role of truth is not to increase your pain. The role of truth is not to chain you to an unwanted reality. Instead, the role of truth is to foster an attitude of acceptance, where you can "know the truth and the truth will set you free," as Jesus says in John 8:32.

You may not want to be set free to live in the truth, desiring rather to be chained to your illusion. This may be what you want, but it is not what you need. You need to live in the truth so you can begin to release all of the pent-up anger, frustration, bitterness, and rage in your life. Truth gives anger a hearing. Truth brings anger out in the open and gives pain a voice.

Once the truth causing the anger has been accepted—truly accepted—and absorbed into your life, the anger should begin to dissipate. You cannot live the life God intended for you full of anger and rage. Listen again to the kind of life God intends for you to live, from Galatians 5:22–23. God wants you to live a life full of "love, joy, peace, patience, kindness, goodness, faithfulness, gentleness and self-control." Anger and rage are nowhere on that list.

The Many Sides of Truth

When Jesus was brought by the Jewish leaders before Pilate, to ask Pilate to kill him for them, he carried on a conversation with Jesus that ended with Pilate's famous question, "What is truth?" (John 18:38). That was a big question. The truth of Jesus before Pilate had to do with the truth of the motives of the Jewish leaders, the truth of Pilate's own culpability, and the truth of Jesus's innocence. It also had to do with the truth of sin itself and the truth of God's plan for salvation. Often, truth is multifaceted, and all the elements of the bigger, wider picture are not always evident.

This can be true of the truth behind your anger. The strength of your anger may be so intense it overshadows the other aspects of the truth of your situation. Acceptance only comes when the whole truth is examined, acknowledged, and integrated into your life. If you've ever watched criminal dramas, you've seen witnesses being sworn in to testify. They are required to pledge to give "the truth, the whole truth, and nothing but the truth." Is this just the verbal excess of anything having to do with a legal proceeding, or is there something to this pledge?

Accepting the truth in your life means you must come to accept the truth, the whole truth, and nothing but the truth. First, there comes an acceptance of the truth in your life that is causing you pain and is a source of your anger. This is the first step in the acceptance process, but it is by no means the last. Next, you need to examine the whole truth. Often, this requires you to look at the situation outside of your experience and witness the truth from differing points of view. After you've taken in these multifaceted perspectives, it's time to examine the truth in its entirety. As you come to see a wider picture of the whole truth, some of what you've come to accept as truth may need to be modified. Some of what you've come to believe may need to be jettisoned. You must determine to accept nothing but the truth. You may find you have layered your truth with opinions, perceptions, reactions, and conclusions that are not, in fact, consistent with the whole truth.

Arriving at truth is a process, especially the more deeply you hurt. It isn't something that can be rushed. It rarely comes neatly packaged in a single revelation. Instead, the Master begins at a single point and proceeds over time to produce an acceptance of the truth, brushstroke by brushstroke, revelation by revelation, understanding by understanding.

It can be difficult to wait, especially when you're in pain. You may want God to produce an instant miracle. You may want to be at the point of acceptance right now, immediately. But if the change was instantaneous, would it alter the substance of the miracle? Could it be that God's miracle is changing you not merely on the surface but all the way down throughout your being?

Think about the miracle of a new life. It isn't instantaneous, although God could certainly have made it that way. Instead, life happens over time, as each part is woven together inside the womb, as Psalm 139 so beautifully depicts. Think about the miracle of aging. People aren't born adults, they are born as babies who age and grow and mature. Again, it's a process. Think about the miracle of spiritual rebirth. It is a process of renewal that Paul talks about in Romans 12:2. God is the God of miracle, but he is also the God of process, and sometimes it's impossible to separate the two. Perhaps it's because you and I would fail to fully understand and appreciate certain miracles if they happened too fast. Process allows for reflection and time to think and appreciate.

I say all of this to help you consider that the very act of acceptance is one that will take time. It is unrealistic of you to expect God to zap you into acceptance in the blink of an eye. It is unfair to expect yourself to fast-forward through this process at some predetermined rate. Instead, accept the process as you learn to accept the truth in your life. Some truths will take longer to absorb and integrate than others. This is because some hurts are deeper and more impacting than others. Your focus should not be on the time it is taking but rather on the progress you are making. Don't doubt the process. Trust that God is at work within you (Phil. 2:13; Eph. 3:20), bringing you to a knowledge of the truth (1 Tim. 2:4).

Note to Self

Whether you think about them or articulate them on a regular basis, you operate in the world based on a set of truths you believe. These truths are rooted in your experiences and what you've come to accept, based on those experiences. These are the truths you wrote down and worked through in chapter 3. I'd like you to go back to that exercise in chapter 3 and take a look at what you wrote down.

Based on the work you've done, revisit your list of truths. You wrote down a list of what you wanted to be true and why. This list and these reasons lie at the heart of your anger. It's time to reexamine them, to find out the truth, the whole truth, and nothing but the truth.

Start with your list of things you wanted to be true from the end of chapter 3. Add any others that have come to mind since you did the exercise in chapter 3.

My List of Truths

1.

2.

3.

4.

5.

Next, I'd like you to think about what the whole truth is surrounding your truths. What else factors into these truths? What perspective have you missed? Think about each truth and begin to fill in around the edges.

The Whole Truth

1.

2.

3.

4.

5.

As you look at each of your truths individually and begin to factor in different perspectives, you may discover other things have been added. These are often negativity stemming from guilt, shame, and fear that attach themselves to your truth, attempting to hijack it and divert you from coming to acceptance. These are thoughts, impressions, and feelings you need to identify and jettison, as they will only weigh you down and anchor you to your anger. What are they? Identify them clearly so you'll be on the alert for their influences.

Something But the Truth

1.

2.

3.

4.

5.

Finally, I'd like you to ask Pilate's question of God, as you look at each of these. I'd like you ask God, "What is truth?" when it comes to your understanding of each. Pray about each one. Write down what you already know about God and about his nature that speaks to you about God's truth and perspective on each. Go ahead and write down where these truths are found or verses that are meaningful to you. In this way, you can go back and revisit these verses.

God's Perspective

1.

2.

3.

4.

5.

While truth is multifaceted, there is only one reality. God, who is able to see things from all sides and understand the long view, knows that reality. He is able to reveal it to you and strengthen you to come to a place of acceptance in your life. Whatever void is in your life, he is able to fill it. Whatever pain is in your life, he is able to comfort it. Whatever guilt is in your life, he is able to forgive it. Whatever shame is in your life, he is able to cover it. Whatever fear is in your life, he is able to relieve it.

Help me! I have stood at the precipice of my anger for so long, afraid to dive in and resolve it. I confess I have not wanted to deal with the truth of my anger because I am afraid. Give me courage, Father, to accept the truth—the whole truth and nothing but the truth. Help me to learn to accept the truth and to accept myself, who I am because of the truth. I thank you that truth is not confined to the bad things I have experienced but the whole truth is bigger, containing your grace, mercy, love, and forgiveness. You have accepted me, Father. Give me the power to accept myself so my life can be a testimony to your glory.

$$\equiv 10 \equiv$$

Experiencing the Power of Forgiveness

Bear with each other and forgive whatever grievances you may have against one another. Forgive as the Lord forgave you.

Colossians 3:13

Some things cannot be mitigated. They cannot be fixed. They cannot be removed. They can only be forgiven. Forgiveness isn't a feeling. It is a strategic, purposeful response to pain and injury—one that can be acted on even if you don't *feel* like it. For some things, only the healing waters of forgiveness have the power to douse the flames of anger. Extending forgiveness is one of the hardest things to do in life. Yet, it brings you closer to the character of God.

Gina could hear the frustration in her sister's voice, mixed with incredulity and a dash of betrayal. "I don't understand how you can stand to be around her! How can you forget what she was like growing up?"

"I haven't *forgotten* what she was like," Gina replied. "I've *forgiven* her for what she was like." It wasn't the first time Gina and her sister had replayed this conversation. It seemed to surface after major holidays. Patricia refused to engage in anything more than a yearly cursory visit while Gina made a point to spend time with their mother. Patricia clearly couldn't stand to be around her mother for longer than was absolutely necessary, and she didn't understand how Gina could. More than once, Patricia implied that Gina was taking sides against her and for their mother.

"Well, maybe you've forgiven her, but I haven't," Patricia announced, feeling strongly she was the one in the right. "If she came to me and admitted how she'd screwed up my life, maybe then I'd think about forgiving her, but she never has and never will."

Gina thought a minute and tried once again to get her sister to understand. "Look, Trish, at her age, Mom is not going to change. She's not going to be anyone other than who she is. She's had a hard life, and it affected her ability to love and take care of us as kids. I guess I just got to a point in my own life where I had to let go of my anger over the way she was."

"I just don't see how you could let that go. Even if I could let go of the past, she's still the same old Mom—negative, judgmental, and critical. I can't remember the last time she had a good thing to say about me. I just can't be around her. She drives me nuts!" Patricia was the older of the two girls and always seemed to take the brunt of their mother's negativity. Gina understood it was harder for her to forgive. The bitterness in Patricia's voice was evident. "I just don't see how you can stand to be around her."

"Once I forgave her, it took away a lot of her power to 'drive me nuts.' I'm not mad at her anymore over the past, so when she starts into that behavior now, I'm able to set really good boundaries. I let her know what I will and won't accept. I'm not saying it's perfect, but she's learning I really mean it. I've left early a couple of times when she wouldn't stop her nagging, but I called her as soon as I got home, just like I always do."

"How do you forgive someone who hasn't asked for it?" Patricia asked, shaking her head as if that settled the question.

"I can forgive her because it's really my decision, not hers," Gina responded. "I need to forgive her more than she wants to be forgiven. I just didn't want to live with all that anger and bitterness inside anymore. The only way to let it go was to forgive."

Patricia looked at Gina as if she'd grown two heads. It didn't make any sense to her, but it made perfect sense to Gina. One of these days, Gina hoped and prayed, it would make perfect sense to Patricia too.

Forgiveness is an odd act. You accept and acknowledge the pain someone has caused. By this you establish blame. You establish they were wrong, for there is no reason to forgive someone who hasn't wronged you. By establishing blame, you declare power over the other person. They now *owe* you for the wrong they caused, whether or not they choose to admit it. The very act of forgiveness establishes the power of blame while at the same time lets it go. It's not an act that makes a lot of sense in many respects.

Letting go of your anger is a process, and forgiveness is often the last stop on the journey. Forgiveness requires that you release the wrong—the source and power of your anger. You cannot truly forgive yet retain your anger. If you're still angry, you haven't really forgiven. Forgiveness, then, can be viewed as increasing your vulnerability because it releases some of the power you've built up with your anger. For many women I've worked with, the thought of letting go of this power is the last option on their list.

Forgiveness is a release, but it is not a release of your personal power. Rather it is a release of your anger and a restoration of your true power. If forgiveness was a release of power, then God would be powerless, for God forgives. In the paradoxical nature of spiritual things, when God forgives us, instead of releasing his power over us, he draws us even closer to himself.

In the last chapter on acceptance, you were reminded that your ways and God's ways are not the same. This reality is vividly brought to mind for me when I think about the act of forgiveness. It is counterintuitive by human standards. Yet, forgiveness is the standard by which God deals with us. Listen to the words of Jesus recorded in Luke 6:36–38: "Be merciful, just as your Father is merciful. Do not judge, and you will not be judged. Do not condemn, and you will not be condemned. Forgive, and you will be forgiven. Give, and it will be given to you. A good measure, pressed down, shaken together and running over, will be poured into your lap. For with the measure you use, it will be measured to you." This reciprocal nature of forgiveness is repeated by Jesus in the passage of Scripture known as the Lord's Prayer, where the forgiveness you seek from God is tied to the forgiveness you show to others (Luke 11:4).

I'm not sure there is a theological concept harder for me to grasp than forgiveness. At the same time, there are few things more achingly beautiful than watching forgiveness unfold. I may not always understand it, but forgiveness always moves me when I witness or experience it. Because it is so difficult at times to grasp and really put into practice, forgiveness over the years has been an important subject and a significant part of what I do in counseling.

Crossing Over

Forgiveness can be a large chasm to cross; the deeper the pain, the wider the gap. Crossing that chasm means leaving behind your anger and resentment. Over the years, there have been women reluctant to do this. They know and understand the world of anger and resentment on one side but are not so sure what the world will be like on the side of forgiveness. They are afraid if they leave anger behind, pain will follow. They want assurances that if they forgive, they won't be hurt again. Because life doesn't come with that sort of guarantee, forgiveness can be a tough sell. Here are some of the questions I've heard from those wanting to cross over to forgiveness but are afraid to. Perhaps these questions mirror some of your own:

Why should I forgive? As I said at the beginning of this chapter, forgiveness is an intentional act, based on decision and not necessarily on feeling. Intentionality says there is a reason to forgive. The reason lies not in the other person but in you. The reason to forgive is not because the other person has wronged you; the reason to forgive is because you decide it is in your best interests to do so. You forgive for your own sake, as well as the sake of the other person.

Isaiah 43:25 records a statement about forgiveness from God. He says: "I, even I, am he who blots out your transgressions, for my own sake, and remembers your sins no more." "For my own sake" is the reason God gives for why he forgives. God chooses to act according to his own nature and for his own sake when he forgives. He chooses to be merciful, loving, and forgiving.

Did you know there is an essential nature that God wants for you? It was mentioned in the last chapter, from Galatians 5:22–23. He wants you to be a person full of "love, joy, peace, patience, kindness, goodness, faithfulness, gentleness and self-control." In all my years of counseling, I have concluded that this is an absolute hunger expressed by women whose lives are out of control with anger. The anger that results from pain and injury in your life wars against this life that God intends. The only way to release the anger, to claim this life, is to practice the art of forgiveness.

Do you remember the image from the last chapter about the master artisan? From the Isaiah verse, you see that forgiveness can blot out the ugly mess sin produces in your life, including anger, bitterness, and resentment. That is why, for your own sake, you need to forgive.

Forgiveness can be like a flower, the benefits of which open to fullness over time. You need to allow time to see the benefits of forgiveness, both psychological and physical. A recent study, reported in the *International Journal of Psychophysiology*, showed an intriguing window into the benefits of forgiveness, which included improved physical symptoms such as heart rate and blood pressure, as well as decreased need for medication and reduced alcohol use. In an abstract on the report, found on the National Institutes of Health website, it says, "These findings have important theoretical implications regarding the forgiveness-health link, suggesting that the benefits of forgiveness extend beyond the dissipation of anger."[3] Forgiveness is a gift you give others, but it is first a gift you give to yourself.

How much do I have to forgive? Forgiveness, like acceptance, is a process. Forgiveness, as a process, has its own built-in momentum. Once you begin to forgive and see the benefits in your life, it makes it easier to forgive the next time. For just about everyone I've worked with, however, there is a wrong in their life resistant to forgiveness. A woman will forgive a hundred other wrongs but come up against a barrier forgiving a certain wrong. The question then arises, *How much do I have to forgive?*

There is actually an answer to this question in Scripture. Jesus and the disciples had a discussion on forgiveness recorded in Matthew 18. During the discussion, Peter asks Jesus, "How many times shall I forgive my brother?" (Matt. 18:21). It seems to Peter that seven times would be an acceptable number— seven, that's quite a bit. Jesus answers and tells him not seven but seventy times seven (18:22). Does this mean that Jesus is saying you are to forgive the 490th time but not the 491st? No, it's not about numbers but about attitude.

To help explain what he means, Jesus tells a parable about an ungrateful servant who, upon being forgiven a massive debt by his master, goes on to hold a fellow servant accountable for a much smaller debt. The master, on hearing of the attitude of the first servant, refuses to forgive the original debt and holds the servant fully accountable (Matt. 18:23–34). Jesus concludes his parable by saying in verse 35, "This is how my heavenly Father will treat each of you unless you forgive your brother from your heart."

Do I have to forgive someone who hasn't asked for forgiveness or acknowledged their need for forgiveness? This is a very difficult question and one that comes up regularly because of the human capacity for denial. People who do wrong can have a stubborn refusal to see it, accept it, and take responsibility for it. Again,

Jesus's discussion about forgiveness in Matthew 18 provides direction on approaching others about forgiveness.

When someone wrongs you, Jesus says you are to go to that person and explain the wrong done to you. If the person does not respond, you go back with one or two other people and try again. If the person still refuses to acknowledge the wrong, Jesus says you are to let the community know. (Here Jesus speaks of the faith community, the church.) After all of this, if the person does not accept responsibility, he or she is to be rejected by that community, as if a "pagan or a tax collector" (Matt. 18:17).

What do you do, then, with the person who refuses to respond to the wrong done, to acknowledge it or accept responsibility for it? Again, I believe the answer lies with you. Like Gina in the story at the beginning of the chapter, your need to forgive may outweigh the other person's desire for forgiveness. If the anger from the wrong is poisoning your life with rage, bitterness, and resentment, for your own sake, you need to forgive so you can let it go. Forgiveness is about your healing, not theirs.

Remember, however, the rest of the discussion from Matthew 18 and the parable of the servant. It can be easier to forgive when you appreciate how much you have been forgiven yourself. Forgiveness is a gift of healing you give to others, often after receiving it for yourself. In the parable, there is no doubt whatsoever that the ungrateful servant is genuinely owed a debt by the second servant. Payment is due. However, the master is angry at the first servant for not extending to the second servant the forgiveness he himself had received. Because all people do wrong things, all people will have both a need for forgiveness and a reason to forgive.

Some wrongs are plainly visible, without qualification. However, other wrongs can be in the eye of the beholder. What one person interprets as a wrong may not appear that way to the other person. When determining whether or not you have been wronged, consider yourself first. If you have formed a "thin skin" because of built-up anger and resentment, you may also have developed a critical spirit, a quick trigger for that anger. This critical spirit may cause you to see people and events through a lens of judgment and offense. If you are quick to judge and easily offended, you are probably easily angered. This anger that springs up almost unbidden can make you feel entitled and empowered. From this platform, even small things take on much larger outlines and obscure the truth of the situation.

While there are some people who will see no need for forgiveness out of denial, others may not see a need for forgiveness because they do not see their action as wrong in the first place. Before you determine to spend the time and energy to inform them of their wrong, you may want to consider another of Jesus's parables. This parable is often referred to as the speck in the eye parable.

Right after Jesus encourages his hearers to "be merciful, just as your Father is merciful" (Luke 6:36), he cautions his disciples on finding fault with other people. He says if you want to point out a speck in someone else's eye, it's better to first take the plank out of your own eye. This goes back to the truth, the whole truth, and nothing but the truth. Is it the truth the other person has a speck in their eye? Yes, it is true. However, the whole truth is, while they've got a speck, you've got a plank. Until you get that plank out of your own eye, you won't be much good at helping the other person with their speck.

You need to be open to the possibility that the other person does not accept responsibility or acknowledge the wrong done because he or she does not see it as a wrong in the first place.

If you want to be clear in order to help them understand it, look first to yourself and evaluate the truth of the situation. In a majority of misunderstandings and fractured relationships, I've found there are generally enough specks and planks to go around. While there are instances where one person is clearly and unequivocally in the wrong, for a large number of other instances, there is simply shared blame. If you can acknowledge your own failures in the situation—your own "plank"—it may be easier for the other person to admit to their "speck."

For some of you, the wrong done to you is not debatable. If the person refuses to accept responsibility and acknowledge their need for forgiveness, you may choose to bestow forgiveness, for your own sake. This does not mean, however, that you are required to continue in relationship with that person. Your withdrawal of relationship, as outlined by Jesus's example in Matthew 18, is a natural consequence of their refusal. Perhaps, at some point, their desire for a restored relationship will draw them into repentance. If so, Jesus says you will have "won" back that person (Matt. 18:15). You can choose to forgive that person and still withhold relationship until you see a change of heart.

You do not know but what your act of forgiveness may start a chain reaction that leads to repentance and a restored relationship. Just because you do not see the cascade effect immediately does not mean it won't happen. You know forgiveness and prayer will produce a change in your own life; they may yet produce a change in the other person's life. In a wonderful book by Nancy Lee DeMoss called *Choosing Forgiveness: Your Journey to Freedom*, she says, "Even when you can't see the results of forgiveness, you can still know you've done what God requires of you."[4] Forgiveness, as a divine act, calls on tremendous changing power, for you and, if accepted, for the other person.

If I forgive someone, does that mean I have to let them hurt me? Any time you remain in relationship with another person, the potential exists for injury; again, because people are flawed. Forgiveness allows for restoration of relationship. I guess I'd like to be able to give you some sort of guarantee that if you forgive someone, it means that person will never hurt you again, but I can't.

However, when a relationship is restored through forgiveness, it allows you the opportunity to restate your boundaries for the relationship. By redrawing and strengthening those boundaries, you may not avoid all pain, but you can call attention to potential problems more quickly and clearly. It takes time for people to change. Once a person understands how his or her behavior is hurtful to you, it may not be possible to "stop on a dime." Instead, their ability to change may require some time, patience, and additional forgiveness on your part.

For my part, I am thankful that God does not require immediate change in order to forgive. He allows you to work toward your goal of becoming like Jesus, forgiving you and accepting you all along the way. He does this because he is realistic about who you are and clear on who he is. Because he desires a relationship with you, he is merciful and forgiving, even beyond the 491st time you need his forgiveness.

If someone asks me for forgiveness, am I required to give it? As you've read in the Matthew 18 passage, the answer is yes. God does require you to give forgiveness to those who ask you for it. The measure of the forgiveness you show to others is the measure God will use in his forgiveness to you. I can't speak for you, but I know I am constantly going to God in order to confess wrongs I've committed against him. Every time I ask for forgiveness, he gives it to me. First John 1:9 promises of God, "If we confess our sins, he is faithful and just and will forgive us our sins and purify us from all unrighteousness." If God is faithful in forgiveness to you, then you must be faithful in forgiveness to others. This is reinforced in the Colossians 3:13 verse that began this chapter.

Can I forgive someone I no longer have a relationship with? If you have not forgiven someone for a wrong they have done against you, you still have a relationship with that person. It is a relationship based on the wrong. Often, it is a relationship based on your anger over that wrong. Even if you never see or speak to that person again, the wronged relationship exists.

This is especially true for adult children who were wronged by a deceased parent or relative. Though the person has died, the anger and resentment have not. Because there is now no way to attain the satisfaction of an acknowledgment of guilt, this pain can fester, producing diversionary anger since the original target is no longer available.

Of what value is living-dead anger or unresolved resentment? If the other person is dead but the anger relationship still hovers around the pain, it is in your best interest to find a way to forgive that person and let them go. If forgiveness is elusive, given the depth of the pain, try first for some level of understanding.

In situations such as these, I've asked women I'm working with to envision the offending person as an infant or small child. No matter how damaging that person was as an adult, he or she started out life as a child. Somewhere, in the pain and dysfunction of life and people, something went terribly wrong. The little soul that started out life so innocent and precious became warped and twisted. That kind of damage is a tremendous loss. It is a tragedy in which the woman herself becomes ensnared because of the wrong done to her by that warped person. Sometimes, this envisioning has the ability to open up a crack in the pain and resentment and allow a sliver of understanding and forgiveness to work its way through.

If the other person is no longer in your life, it is still possible for you to work through to forgiveness and let the pain go. Often, you will also need to release some deeply held desire for the truth of your life to be different than what it is, for the person to be someone other than who they are. Releasing yourself and the past to the truth is the only way to see it for what it is so you can truly let it go.

If I'm partially to blame, does that cancel out the need for forgiveness? This is often a line of reasoning used by those who have wronged you. If it is not possible to completely deny the wrong done, he or she may attempt to shift blame by bringing up real or imagined wrongs on your part. In an effort to shift blame, the person simply tries to spread more around. This is a common tactic and not one to be sucked into. Each person is responsible for their own actions. Each wrong stands on its own.

If you were in the wrong, you need to acknowledge the truth, accept it, and ask forgiveness. However, this does not negate the need for the other person to do likewise. Beware of those who attempt to assign blame for small or minor things in order to defend themselves against larger, more egregious wrongs. If this happens, the person is not openly and honestly accepting responsibility. They are not ready to embrace the truth. Once they can accept responsibility for their actions without raising collateral issues, then they are ready.

What happens if I don't want to forgive someone? If that is how you really feel, it would do little good to hide it. Instead, you need to be honest with yourself and admit where you are in this process. Forgiveness is something that needs to be worked on, thought about, and prayed over. The deeper the hurt, the longer it may take to come to forgiveness.

This is a matter between you and God, for forgiveness is a divine attribute. It is a Spirit-directed response. Be open with yourself, with God, and with the other person about this journey you are on to forgiveness. Claim for yourself Ephesians 4:2, which says that we are to be humble and gentle, patient with one another, bearing with one another in love. Their very acceptance of your need for time, and the patience to give you that time, may help you arrive at your destination of forgiveness sooner. If the other person can set aside their own need for forgiveness right now and allow you the time you need to process through to forgiveness, this indicates an ability to consider your needs above their own. This is an excellent sign that the person has done their own work toward a restored and renewed relationship.

What about the role of repentance in forgiveness? Just as you may need patience in coming to forgiveness, the other person may need time to come to a place of repentance. One of the hardest things to do is to admit you have wronged another person and caused pain. Understanding the depth of the wrong and the amount of the pain can take time to assimilate. Taking time to get there does not mean repentance won't happen at all; it means coming to an understanding of the need for repentance is a process.

This is how God deals with you. As you learn more about who he is and the nature of his holiness, the more you come to realize how substandard your actions are. However, God does not condemn you for this but gives you time to come to repentance. Listen to these reassuring words from 2 Peter 3:9: "The Lord is not slow in keeping his promise, as some understand slowness. He is patient with you, not wanting anyone to perish, but everyone to come to repentance." Repentance allows reconciliation and a rebirth of relationship. This is a noble and worthy goal. Therefore, repentance is worth waiting for. In an ideal situation, as you journey toward a point of forgiveness, the other person is working toward a full understanding of their need for repentance. Reconciliation and relationship renewal occur at the crossroads of forgiveness and repentance.

Sadly, there are some people who will never truly repent of the wrongs they have done to you. They are blinded by their own denial and self-deception. This will, undoubtedly, retard your journey to forgiveness, but you must not allow it to derail you. If repentance is not possible for that person, understanding and forgiveness is possible for you. The other person may choose to remain mired in deception and denial, but you can free yourself from your anger and bitterness.

Am I required to forgive the truly evil? It is not possible to forgive evil. Evil must be named and fought against. Evil should never be explained away or downplayed. Evil has devastating consequences. It is opposite of God. The two cannot be joined through forgiveness. Evil cannot be forgiven; it must be exposed and dealt with.

Having said that, I want you to consider the distinction between evil itself and people who do evil things. In the book of Ezekiel, there is a passage that speaks about the evil people do. It might be easy to conclude that evil people are evil and should be completely written off because of that evil. That is not, however, what Scripture says.

Please read the following passage, especially thinking about the people who have committed acts of evil against you. These are the people you will find it easiest to write off and hardest to forgive. This passage gives God's perspective:

> But if a wicked man turns away from all the sins he has committed and keeps all my decrees and does what is just and right, he will surely live; he will not die. None of the offenses

he has committed will be remembered against him. Because of the righteous things he has done, he will live. Do I take any pleasure in the death of the wicked? declares the Sovereign Lord. Rather, am I not pleased when they turn from their ways and live?

Ezekiel 18:21–23

No, evil cannot be forgiven; but people who do evil things can. People who do evil things can be forgiven when they repent and turn from their wicked ways, as 2 Chronicles 7:14 says. For those people who have committed acts of evil against you, your anger can be stoked by a desire for retribution. God's example, however, is to desire not retribution but repentance. God says he is pleased when evil people turn from their wicked ways and live.

In thinking of repentance or retribution, you need to be more like God and less like Jonah. Jonah was sent by God to go to the city of Nineveh to preach repentance to the people there. You'd think a prophet like Jonah would be thrilled at such an assignment. However, Jonah rebelled, and what happened next has to do with a rather large fish and some time in a dark place for Jonah to rethink his opposition to God's will.

Even after being vomited up onto dry land after his stay in the belly of the fish, Jonah is still angry at God (Jonah 4:1). Why is he angry? Jonah is angry because he wants retribution, not repentence, for the city of Nineveh, an enemy of his nation of Israel. He wants to see Nineveh destroyed, not salvaged. Sitting out in the desert, pouting, Jonah is upset and angry, complaining that God is a "gracious and compassionate God, slow to anger and abounding in love, a God who relents from sending calamity" (4:2). These are normally attributes you would frame as praise to God, not as part of an angry outburst!

In order for Jonah to see the whole truth of the situation, God sends a vine to grow up over Jonah's head in the desert to give him shade. Then, just as quickly as the vine grows up, God sends a worm to chew into the vine, causing it to wither and die. Jonah is now angry about the vine as well. God asks Jonah in verse 9 if he has any right to be angry about the vine, to which Jonah answers, "I do. I am angry enough to die." Jonah is just mad about everything. He's mad about the vine, he's mad that God wants to save Nineveh instead of destroy it, and he's mad that God wants him to be an agent of repentance and not retribution. He's so angry, he just wants to die.

Jonah's had his say, now it's time for him to hear God's perspective: "But the LORD said, 'You have been concerned about this vine, though you did not tend it or make it grow. It sprang up overnight and died overnight. But Nineveh has more than a hundred and twenty thousand people who cannot tell their right hand from their left, and many cattle as well. Should I not be concerned about this great city?'" (Jon. 4:10–11). God invites Jonah to put down his anger and pick up God's compassion, even for those people caught in wickedness.

No, evil cannot be forgiven, but people who are caught in evil can be. They can be thought of with compassion. They can be prayed over and intervened for, that God would bring about a miracle in their lives to lead them to repentance. Detest the evil they have done while you find a way to have compassion for the horror they have chosen, the evil that so warps their minds and blinds their eyes they are unable to tell their right hand from their left.

It is God's plan and purpose that everyone should come to repentance and live, including the very people who have committed acts of wrong and evil against you. Evil cannot be redeemed, but people who have done evil can be. This is God's work of redemption. With all my heart I pray that you will be able to know and experience such a change of heart by those who have wronged you and committed evil against you. May you be joined to them not merely in the evil that took place but in the repentance and reconciliation made possible through God's work of redemption.

Forgiving Yourself

How do I forgive myself? I have been surprised over the years at how often the women who display the most love and forgiveness to others fail to extend the same blessing to themselves. Instead, they bless others while they curse themselves. This is not what God intends. James 3:10 says it is not right that out of the same mouth should come both blessing and cursing. He was speaking of the mouth being used to bless God and curse others. I believe this also applies to blessing others with forgiveness and cursing yourself with unremitting blame, shame, and guilt.

In the previous chapter, you read about the curse of perfectionism. Perfectionism never gives you a day off. It never lets up its unyielding demands. It never allows you to forgive yourself and move forward. Relentless, it provides no respite. The pressure to perform, to be perfect, is inexorable. It never lets up.

This pressure leads to rage and despair. This anger is often directed outward, but it is also directed inward. Perfectionism causes you to curse yourself. Learning how to forgive yourself diffuses the curse of perfectionism. As such, it is a blessing. God, who loves you, does not want you to live a life cursing yourself.

Rather, he wants you to accept and love yourself, being kind, gentle, and forgiving.

There is another side to giving up perfectionism that must be acknowledged and accepted. As you've read before, if you admit that you are not perfect, you may be giving up a tightly held strategy for attaining a dream or living out an illusion of the past. I urge you, let it go. The perfection you seek is truly an illusion; it did not exist then, it doesn't exist now, and it never will. The more you strive for it, the farther it fades away. Let it go so you will have room in your heart to embrace the truth—the whole truth and nothing but the truth.

If you find it easier to forgive others than yourself, practice. Because you blame yourself for so much, you'll have plenty of opportunity to practice! Practice over and over again. Consider the words of God spoken to Jonah. The people of Nineveh, imperfect though they were, were loved by God. Like the vine, he tended each one of those one hundred and twenty thousand souls and made them grow. He was concerned for them. You, also, are not perfect. You, also, are loved by God, tended gently by him. It is God who formed you in your mother's womb (Psalm 139) and made you grow. God is concerned about you. He loves you and wants you to learn to forgive yourself, just as he has already forgiven you.

Note to Self

It is time to practice forgiveness. I'd like you to start by practicing on yourself. Think back over your life and consider the times when you know you were at fault, where your actions and attitudes were hurtful. Start with those actions and attitudes that were hurtful to others. It is not up to me to delineate what sort of things to put on your list. These are times for you to determine, based on how you feel and what you have heard from others. Be honest about your own actions and it will help you later to put the actions of others in context.

Be specific. Write down when, what happened, and, from your perspective, why it happened. You may choose to indicate a specific incident or a general pattern of behavior that you believe was harmful to another. Open yourself up to regret. As you think back over your life and look honestly at your present, what are you truly sorry for? Now, write those down.

Why I Need Forgiveness from Others

1.
2.
3.
4.
5.

Looking back over your list, ask yourself if you have taken the steps to go to that person and ask for forgiveness. If you have, what was the outcome? If you have not, indicate what stopped you from seeking forgiveness. Was it fear, anger, shame, guilt? Name the barrier.

My Path Toward Forgiveness

1.
2.
3.
4.
5.

For the barriers, I want you to come up with an action plan to begin work at overcoming each. This work should include steps such as these:

- Engage in personal prayer.
- Ask for the prayers of others who are trustworthy and able to join you in overcoming this barrier.
- Determine how you should approach that person and ask for forgiveness. It may be necessary for you to gain wise counsel on the best way to do this, through working with a trusted friend, pastoral counselor, or professional therapist.
- Be accountable to go through with your plan to seek forgiveness from that other person.

It is possible, for some of you, that the person you need to ask forgiveness from is no longer available to you. Either they have withdrawn relationship from you completely or they are no longer alive. In this case, the forgiveness you seek from them will have to come instead from you. You will need to seek and grant forgiveness to and from yourself.

In addition to wrongs you have done to others for which you must now ask forgiveness from and give forgiveness to yourself, you must consider the ways in which you have intentionally caused harm to yourself, with no other person involved. Often, the person you are the hardest on and for whom you have the least amount of pity and compassion is yourself. It is time to forgive and learn to truly love yourself again.

Think of the relationship you have with yourself, including all those conversations you have with yourself for which no one else is privy. There are things you hold against yourself, things you blame yourself for, things you hate yourself for. Just as God does not want you to live in hate of others, he does not want you to live in hate for yourself. The commandment to love your neighbor is predicated on the love you have for yourself (Lev. 19:18). From this commandment, not only are you to love your neighbor, you are also to love yourself.

I Need to Forgive Myself For:

1.

2.

3.

4.

5.

God's forgiveness and compassion are for everyone, including you. He wants all people to come to repentance and forgiveness, including you. He promises that if you ask, he will forgive you (Eph. 1:7). If God is able to forgive your sins, you cannot hold back your own forgiveness. To do so negates the work of Christ and goes against the very nature and plan of God. Release your guilt and shame. Accept God's forgiveness and allow it to empower your own. Begin to see yourself through God's eyes—as a precious child and soul, grown and tended by him, for whom he has great and eternal compassion.

As you come to an understanding of and an appreciation for God's forgiveness and a greater ability to forgive yourself, I'd like you to think about those who have wronged you. Consider if reconciliation is possible. Ask yourself the following questions about that person:

- Does this person accept responsibility for the wrong done to me?
- Have I ever spoken to this person and explained the depth of my pain?

- If I have, what was the outcome?
- If I have not, what is stopping me from doing so?
- If I have not, can I see a way to do this in the present or future?
- If this person is no longer available to me, what will it take for me to forgive?
- Does this person need more time to come to repentance? If so, am I willing to give this person that time?
- If this person does not understand or see the wrong done to me, am I willing to forgive and move past the hurt in order to continue in relationship with this person? If I am not willing now, what will it take for me to be willing in the future?
- What can I be doing today to make repentance and reconciliation more possible in the future?

I would like you to think about what forgiveness and reconciliation would look like in your life. Instead of writing down concrete answers, I'd like you to consider a more artistic response. You can either create a picture or painting, interpreting a life of forgiveness. You might decide to take a series of photographs, depicting the feelings forgiveness creates within you. You might write a poem, using imagery to explain how such a life of forgiveness would feel and look. You might put such a poem to music or create a song. Find a way to cement these feelings in your heart and mind using your artistic, creative side. In some ways, this may touch you more deeply than any other thing you have done in this section. Be open to interpretation and give yourself permission to create.

Keep this expression close to you as you work through the journey to forgiveness. Allow it to motivate, encourage, and empower you to move through barriers. Use it as a reminder to keep you focused and go forward.

Finally, I'd like you to look at yourself in a mirror. I mean, really look at yourself. Look into your own eyes. Think about yourself as that young and precious child, formed by and beloved of God. Then say out loud, "I forgive myself."

Father, forgive me my trespasses, as I forgive those who trespass against me. Help me to have your heart of care and compassion, even against those who have wronged me. Help me to learn how to forgive myself and move beyond the prison of perfectionism. Strengthen my mind to accept weaknesses and my heart to forgive.

Some people, Lord, are my enemies. I see them as such because of what they have done to me. Grant me the heart of Jesus where my enemies are concerned, for I cannot love them, as Jesus calls me to do, without you. Wherever possible, reconcile me to my enemies, even if that enemy is me. Help me to live a life of forgiveness, mercy, and grace.

$$=== 11 ===$$

Living the Power of Optimism, Hope, and Joy

May the God of hope fill you with all joy and peace as you trust in him, so that you may overflow with hope by the power of the Holy Spirit.

Romans 15:13

When you move past your anger and learn to accept yourself and forgive those who have hurt you, you are a powerful woman. You are renewed and reenergized. You are ready to embrace a life devoted to the positive pursuits of optimism, hope, and joy.

Joan glanced up from the book she was reading, having just heard her flight number called out. Paying attention to the overhead announcement, she soon learned her flight was delayed—something about maintenance. A pleasant and professional voice assured listeners the flight would be underway as soon as possible.

She'd already been sitting in the terminal for around an hour, waiting to board. *Okay*, she thought to herself, *might as well get up and walk around.* As she gathered up her purse and carry-on, she could hear several people loudly complaining about the delay. One furious man was already berating the airline attendant at the gate counter, as if she was personally responsible. Not so long ago, she would have wholeheartedly joined him.

Not anymore, Joan promised herself. She was not going to fall into that trap again. Instead, she determined to keep a positive attitude as she made her way to a dutyfree store a short distance up the walkway.

These things happen, she reminded herself. *I'd rather they checked out any maintenance issues than fly a plane that's unsafe.* As soon as she found out what the new time frame would be, she'd call her daughter and let her know so she wouldn't worry.

There were several shops right next to each other, and Joan carefully maneuvered her carry-on through each of them, enjoying the freedom to take her time and examine the wares. It was so rare nowadays that she actually had time to just window-shop. There wasn't anything she could do to fix the plane faster, and getting upset over the unexpected delay would only make the time slow to a crawl.

As she browsed through the selection of books and travel-related gadgets, something triggered in her mind. She'd been meaning to call a friend she hadn't been able to get with for the past several weeks. Checking her watch, Joan did a quick time calculation and figured her friend would probably be home and through with dinner by now. Moving out of the store and making her way back toward her gate, she pulled out her cell phone. On the third ring her friend picked up, delighted at the call. By the time they'd chatted their way through jobs, kids, family, and the latest news, the plane was fixed and would be boarding in fifteen minutes.

There, Joan thought to herself as she dialed her daughter's number. *That wasn't so bad.*

A Full Life

When you intentionally grab hold of and fill your mind with good things like optimism, hope, and joy instead of bad things like anger and bitterness, you are able to change the content of your life. This can be a wonderful and frightening prospect. It is wonderful to consider being different from who you've been. It can also be frightening if you aren't sure if this new person you'll become will be safe.

As you work through these last few chapters, if you are still pondering whether or not, deep down, you really want to give up your anger, I'd like you to ask yourself these questions: *How do I want to feel? What kind of person do I really want to be?*

Anger, rage, bitterness, and resentment are powerful and can take over who you are. They can warp who you are. They can *become* who you are and overshadow how you feel. Again, what kind of person do you really want to be? Jesus said in Luke:

No good tree bears bad fruit, nor does a bad tree bear good fruit. Each tree is recognized by its own fruit. People do not pick figs from thorn bushes, or grapes from briers. The good man brings good things out of the good stored up in his heart, and the evil man brings evil things out of the evil stored up in his heart. For out of the overflow of his heart his mouth speaks.

Luke 6:43–45

You have a choice to make—are you going to store up good things in your heart or are you going to hold on to the bad things? If you hold on to your anger, for whatever reason, you endanger yourself, for it is possible to be overcome by the bad things that happened to you. You must establish a bulwark against the bad by filling yourself up with good things, like optimism, hope, and joy. Good is the only thing powerful enough to withstand evil. Romans 12:21 says, "Do not be overcome by evil, but overcome evil with good." If you don't fill yourself up with good things, you run the risk of being overcome by evil.

I have sat in my office, doing family counseling, watching evil pass down from generation to generation. One family member has been injured in the past by a terrible wrong. That pain produces a wellspring of anger, rage, bitterness, and resentment that spews forth onto the rest of her family. This anger, like hot lava, scalds all of her other relationships. The person who was injured in the first place ends up injuring those she loves. She is overcome by the wrong that happened to her in that she becomes an avenue herself for wrong.

Are you a thorn bush? Is coming into contact with you like running into a brier? When family, friends, or acquaintances come to you for a sweet fig or juicy grape, do they walk away full of barbs and scratches from your prickly personality? If so, you have been overcome by the wrong that happened to you. You are overcome by evil things you have stored up in your heart. You have been storing up the wrong things. You have become a toxic dump site that is poisoning your life. Time for some serious housecleaning.

The Rest of the Story

Removing the anger you have felt for so long is a wonderful thing. It is not, however, the end of the story. Jesus points this out in a cautionary tale, a parable found in Matthew 12:43–45 about removing negative things. He tells the story about an evil spirit who, after leaving a man, wanders aimlessly in desert places without finding rest. At this point, the spirit decides to return: "Then it says, 'I will return to the house I left.' When it arrives, it finds the house unoccupied, swept clean and put in order. Then it goes and takes with it seven other spirits more wicked than itself, and they go in and live there. And the final condition of that man is worse than the first." According to this parable, it is not enough to empty yourself of the bad things. If the void created by the departure of the bad is not filled up with good, the bad may come home again to roost, worse than before.

Coming to the fullness of life is a two-part process. Yes, you must remove the bad, but you must also intentionally seek out and incorporate the good. This can be a challenge for those who have lived a life full of anger. In your head, you know you should not live this way anymore. So, intentionally, you make other choices. But, at some point, your head knowledge of what you must do needs to be followed up by a true change in heart: a softening, a lowering of barriers, and an embrace of the "vulnerable" emotions of optimism, hope, and joy.

Jesus's parable smacks of a perfectionist attitude and highlights the danger therein. In the story, the house is empty, swept clean, and put in order. This could be considered a working definition of perfectionism—pristine, neat, and orderly. As such, it can be a temptation to think of this condition as acceptable, even enviable. After all, the anger is gone, the turbulent reactions are swept clean, and your emotional house is "in order." You may say to yourself, "This is enough. Why must I do anything more?"

An "empty" house, devoid of emotion, may seem a reasonable alternative to the turbulence of your anger. If you believe this to be true, however, you are in real danger according to the parable. The operative word in the parable isn't the perfectionist one of *order*, it's the word *empty*. Empty things have a way of filling up again. And they often fill up with what was there before because the pathways have already been established and the precedent set.

I say this in no way to diminish the work, the hard work, you've done so far of ridding yourself of your anger. Rather, I say this to encourage you to *keep going*! You have not quite crossed the finish line; there is one more thing left for you to do. You have emptied out the anger, now you must invite in the good. In fact, you must stuff your life with so much good, so much positive, you simply have no room left for the negative to return.

Think back to the passage on judging others, found in Luke 6:37–39, that you've looked at before. Here it is again: "Do not judge, and you will not be judged. Do not condemn, and you will not be condemned. Forgive, and you will be forgiven. Give, and it will be given to you. A good measure, pressed down, shaken together and running over, will be poured into your lap. For with the measure you use, it will be measured to you." This is the image I'd like you to have in your mind of how you need to stuff your life with good things: pressed down, shaken together, and running over so there isn't room for anything else. And don't worry—optimism, hope, and joy have the built-in capacity for expansion. They have the ability to fill up your heart and your life so full, even if anger did want to return it couldn't maintain a single hand or foothold.

So, how do you get from an orderly life, where anger is removed, to a packed-full life, where good crams into every nook and cranny? The answer is to be as intentional about what you put into your life as you are about what to remove. For those of you who like lists, here are a couple of really good ones. Consider these as "packing" lists—not packing as in what you're going to remove but packing as in what you're going to pack into your life.

- "But the fruit of the Spirit is love, joy, peace, patience, kindness, goodness, faithfulness, gentleness and self-control" (Gal. 5:22–23). You've seen these verses before, but they cannot be emphasized enough. These are the fruit promised by God through the Holy Spirit. So, if you doubt you'll ever be able to come up with these on your own, relax! You don't have to! You aren't required to manufacture these feelings; they come from God. Rather, you need to be alert to their presence in your life and open to receiving them, to reaching out and grabbing hold of them. These are gifts of God, miraculous and marvelous to behold.
- "Whatever is true, whatever is noble, whatever is right, whatever is pure, whatever is lovely, whatever is admirable—if anything is excellent or praiseworthy—think about such things" (Phil. 4:8). You've seen this passage too, but I place it before you again. It does matter what you think about, not merely what you do. Your actions are important, but it is also critical what thoughts you consent to fill your mind with.

Every person you meet, every circumstance you encounter, is an opportunity to choose how to respond. Each opportunity is a chance for housecleaning. If you discover a negative response or reaction peeking out from the corner of your heart, reject it and choose a positive response instead. Make sure to mark where that negative reaction surfaced so you can work through it and clear it out. Again, think process. You are reorganizing the interior of your heart.

Optimism

In a world jaded by negativity, optimism can appear an anachronism. A throwback to some younger, more naïve time when all the world seemed ripe with wonderful possibilities. Kind of sounds like childhood, doesn't it? And you remember what Jesus said about children in Matthew 19:14, don't you? He said the kingdom of heaven belonged to them, and he warned adults in Matthew 18:3, "Unless you change and become like little children, you will never enter the kingdom of heaven." Optimism may seem a little childish, but it offers a key to the kingdom of heaven.

Optimism is defined as "an inclination to put the most favorable construction upon actions and events or to anticipate the best possible outcome." You could also call this the power of positive thinking. Optimism comes from a heart where good things are stored. Optimism comes from believing that tomorrow holds a blessing and not a curse.

Optimism, however, must not be confused with unfounded, unrealistic wishful thinking. Wishful thinking is based solely on desires. Your optimism should be founded in an understanding of the truth. The truth is that God loves you. There is nothing more foundational than that. This truth is what allowed David to write in the Psalms, "The LORD is with me; I will not be afraid. What can man do to me?" (Ps. 118:6) and "In God I trust; I will not be afraid. What can man do to me?" (56:11).

Anger tends to put the least favorable construction on actions or events and prods you to anticipate the worst possible outcome. When you intentionally decide to be optimistic, you change the pH content of your heart—you go from the acidity of negativism to the alkalinity of being positive. When your heart is full of optimism, negativity finds it harder to set up shop and grow.

In this world, you know, optimism can take a real beating. Negativity flourishes in so many aspects of our culture. That is why optimism cannot be founded on this world. Instead, it must have its anchor in a different place. Optimism must be firmly anchored to hope.

Hope

Hope is defined as expecting with confidence. It's being sure today of what hasn't happened yet. In this world, if optimism is childish, hope can appear outright delusional, especially hope in God. As a Christian, I reject that worldview, "because I know whom I have believed, and am convinced that he is able to guard what I have entrusted to him" (2 Tim. 1:12). As a counselor, I dispute that worldview, for I have seen firsthand the power of hope to change lives and attitudes.

Hope based on the world is an iffy proposition. Hope based on faith in God is rock solid. Hope and faith go hand in hand, like inseparable lovers. Hebrews 11:1 says, "Now faith is being sure of what we hope for and certain of what we do not see." When faith is the basis of your belief in tomorrow, you open yourself up to the power and possibilities of God. When anger is the basis of your belief in tomorrow, you close yourself down to the pain and limits of disappointment.

The world may say that hope is a delusion, but God does not. Psalm 25:3 says that no one whose hope is in God will ever be put to shame. And it's no wonder that this world doesn't put much stock in hope. Hope based on the world is exceedingly untrustworthy. Hope from this world comes to nothing because it is hope based on desires like wealth and power. Proverbs 11:7 warns that "when a wicked man dies, his hope perishes; all he expected from his power comes to nothing." Hope based on this world ultimately comes to nothing.

Hope based on God is made of different metal. It is strong and lasting. This is the hope you need to fill your heart with. When you do, instead of being disappointed, you will be invigorated. Listen to this beautiful passage from Isaiah 40:31: "But those who hope in the LORD will renew their strength. They will soar on wings like eagles; they will run and not grow weary, they will walk and not be faint." Your anger may be based on worldly hope unfulfilled. You may be angry because something you wished for didn't happen. You may be angry because someone who should have treated you better didn't. You may be angry because your life was supposed to turn out differently than it did. This is hope with you as the focus. Instead, turn the focus of your hope to God, and you will not be disappointed or put to shame.

I believe these things myself and have seen them manifested in the lives of others. When I offer them to you, I do so humbly, understanding the depth of pain and the difficulty of hope in your life. To those of you who come from a place of deep suffering, I offer this verse from Isaiah 57:10 as you persevere: "You were wearied by all your ways, but you would not say, 'It is hopeless.' You found renewal of your strength, and so you did not faint." Please don't give up. Instead, give in to hope. Open up your heart to its power and possibilities. Believe God when he says, "'For I know the plans I have for you,' declares the LORD, 'plans to prosper you and not to harm you, plans to give you hope and a future'" (Jer. 29:11).

Hope in God is not wishful thinking. It is hope set on the goal of the good God has for you. It is based on his character of love, forgiveness, and mercy. It is based on the foundation of his plans for you. This type of hope allows you to experience the joy of optimism. Hope allows you to color your world and see it afresh.

When your world is recast in the light of hope, it does not mean that the truth of your life is somehow whitewashed and concealed. Hope does not reject the truth of the past but rather focuses on the promise of the future. Living a life filled with optimism, hope, and joy is not a rejection of your truth. It is not a minimization of your pain. It is an integration of the truth of your life with the redeeming power of God.

When you embrace hope, you embrace God. God, who knows your life, your past, and your pain, is trustworthy to keep that truth for you. God is the one "who redeems your life from the pit and crowns you with love and compassion, who satisfies your desires with good things so that your youth is renewed like the eagle's. The LORD works righteousness and justice for all the oppressed" (Ps. 103:4–6). God knows who you are and what you have suffered. He understands the "pit" you've endured, but you do not need to remain in the pit for it to be acknowledged. God wants you out of the pit, crowned with love and compassion, satisfied with good things in your life so your life is renewed. And while he is doing all of this, he is still working for righteousness and justice on your behalf. You can let those crushing burdens go and allow the almighty God to carry them for you. Free from these burdens, your soul can soar on the wings of optimism, hope, and joy.

Joy

Joy is the noun and rejoice is the verb. Joy is both an attitude and an action. Acts 2:26 bears this out when it says, "Therefore my heart is glad and my tongue rejoices; my body also will live in hope." One of the very best things you can fill your heart up with is a capacity for joy. Joy is an aggressive, proprietary emotion that grabs on to the good and shakes it for all it is worth.

An attitude of rejoicing, besides being the first fruit of the Spirit listed in Galatians, is also an intentional response to life and its circumstances. The apostle Paul puts it pretty succinctly when he says, "Rejoice in the Lord always. I will say it again: Rejoice!" (Phil. 4:4). To rejoice is a planned response, not one based solely on feelings. After all, he says to rejoice *always*. Always covers a lot of ground.

When you choose to be joyful in life, you state ahead of time how you are going to respond to circumstances, situations, and people. It's as if you set joy as your default setting, the home page of your emotions. Joy is the lens you choose to look through now just as anger was the lens you used in the past.

In the past, anger gave you a shot in the arm. You used it to fuel your life and knock down obstacles. Now, you can look to a different source of strength. God is not deceived about what it takes to live in this world. He understands completely that it requires strength to live day by day. Anger offers its services; God chooses a different path. Instead of anger, choose joy. Nehemiah 8:10 says, "Do not grieve, for the joy of the LORD is your strength." David says in Psalm 28:7, "The LORD is my strength and my shield; my heart trusts in him, and I am helped. My heart leaps for joy and I will give thanks to him in song."

This is not an easy thing to do. Optimism, hope, and joy are muscular activities. They run counter to culture and personal preference. As such, engaging in them requires overcoming natural resistance. Optimism, hope, and joy take the power-lifting of faith. Just as a weight lifter learns how to set his or her body and the weight in order to be successful, there are ways in which to handle this kind of heavy lifting. Romans 12:2 says to "be joyful in hope, patient in affliction, faithful in prayer." Each is a component of living out a positive life. You must have an optimistic attitude, based on a firm foundation, while being realistic and patient about your present circumstances as you look to a positive future.

A Considerate Life

Again, you must adopt an optimistic attitude. You must decide how you will respond to what life brings your way. You must take a *considerate* approach. James says that you are to "consider it pure joy" when you face trials. Does this mean that trials and problems, challenges and hardships aren't difficult? No, of course not! But James is speaking of attitude. You are to *consider* these trials as pure joy. You are to think about them in that way; you are to view them through this filter. Think about it this way: if you can reach a point in your life and spiritual maturity where you are able to view trials as cause for pure joy, you will never have a lack of joy in your life, because this life, as Jesus promised, comes with trials.

Why would James ask such an incomprehensible thing? Because he knows that life is about more than just your trials. He goes on to acknowledge that this type of attitude will test your faith but that this testing will produce perseverance. Perseverance leads to maturity and completeness. This is why you have joy—not because of the trial but because of the outcome of the trial, in the fruit produced in your life. When you can take a trial, a wrong done against you, and turn it into an avenue of strength and personal maturity, you declare victory over the wrong. Living a life of joy is a triumph over tragedy, a defeat of the power of evil in your life. This is certainly a cause for celebration and "pure joy"!

As you learn to do this, you strengthen your faith and fortify your hope. Romans 5:3–4 marks the connection this way: "Not only so, but we also rejoice in our sufferings, because we know that suffering produces perseverance; perseverance, character; and character, hope." Optimism, hope, and joy are all interwoven through the fabric of faith. This is the garment God intends for you to wear, and you need to put it on every day.

God Rejoices

As you rid yourself of all anger, bitterness, and malice, and fill yourself up with the fruit of the Spirit, God is pleased. You declare your trust in him and demonstrate your faith. Whenever you forgive and show mercy, you imitate God and model Christ. These are hard things to do; God knows this. Yet, when you do them, you say to the world, "I choose to do things God's way, not your way." In this, God is glorified and your life is praise to him.

Scary as it is, uncomfortable as it is, foreign to you as it is, you will be blessed when you choose God's way. As you learn to rejoice over all sorts of circumstances, God rejoices over you:

"The LORD your God is with you, he is mighty to save. He will take great delight in you, he will quiet you with his love, he will rejoice over you with singing" (Zeph. 3:17). As you put down anger and pick up optimism, hope, and joy, don't be afraid; God is with you and he is able to protect you. He promises to quiet your fears and rejoice over you with joyful singing.

Note to Self

Just as forgiveness takes practice, especially when it comes to forgiving yourself, optimism, hope, and joy take practice. It means looking at life through a different lens than the one you've been using. It means opening up your heart again.

As a start, I'd like you to go back to those "lists" in this chapter—the fruit of the Spirit found in Galatians 5:22–23 and the "whatever" list from Philippians 4:8. From these two lists, I'd like you to come up with an art project. Using whatever medium you'd like—paint, collage, crayons, colored pencils, decoupage, markers—find a way to represent each of these words (love, joy, peace, patience, kindness, goodness, faithfulness, gentleness, self-control, and true, noble, right, pure, lovely, admirable, excellent, praiseworthy) in a way that has meaning and connection to you. Take your time and really think about the exercise, for this piece of art is something I want you to keep with you. I want you to place it in a private place, a place where you can go to be reminded and to meditate on the beauty these things represent. This piece of art is a physical representation of how you want to look to others and to yourself. This piece of art will help you come to a deeper understanding of what God already sees when he looks at you.

After you have done your artwork, return and answer these questions:

- How will my life be different when I am an optimistic, hopeful, and joyful person?

- How will my family life change when I change?

- Of the three—optimism, hope, and joy—which one do I find easiest to incorporate into my life? Why?

- Of the three, which one do I find the hardest to incorporate? Why?

- I confess, I have had difficulty being optimistic in the past because . . .

- I confess, I have had difficulty being hopeful in the past because . . .

- I confess, I have had difficulty being joyful in the past because . . .

In order to incorporate more positive things in my life, I realize I must give up some negative habits, perspectives, and attitudes:

- In order to become more optimistic, I need to get over this one habit:

- In order to become more hopeful, I need to overcome this one perspective:

- In order to become more joyful, I need to give up this one attitude:

- I want to be more optimistic in my life because . . .

- I want to be more hopeful in my life because . . .

- I want to be more joyful in my life because . . .

- In order to be more optimistic, I will do the following:
    1.
    2.
    3.

- In order to be more hopeful, I will do the following:
    1.
    2.
    3.
- In order to be more joyful, I will do the following:
    1.
    2.
    3.

Dear Father, help me to choose to live a life devoted to you, trusting you to protect me and alert to the blessings you bring each day into my life. I want to be able to get up each morning, to say and really believe "this is the day the LORD has made; I will rejoice and be glad in it" (Ps. 118:24). Just as I need your help, your strength, wisdom, and direction to get rid of my anger, to get rid of the bad things in my life, I need your help to fill up my life with good things. I confess I can be suspicious of good things. I confess sometimes I don't want to accept good things because I don't want to feel obligated to change and give up something else. Help me to unclench my hands of the things I think I need in order to be able to grasp hold of what you provide.

Father, you are a God of hope. I claim Romans 15:13 for myself: fill me with all joy and peace as I trust in you, so that I may overflow with hope and the power of the Holy Spirit.

12

Relying on the Power of God

Jesus looked at them and said, "With man this is impossible, but with God all things are possible."

Matthew 19:26

People look out at the majesty of the Grand Canyon or the might of the Pacific Ocean or the grandeur of the Great Smoky Mountains and marvel at the power of God.

They sit out among the stars and look at the heavens and get lost in the vastness of space. Psalm 19:1 says, "The heavens declare the glory of God; the skies proclaim the work of his hands." They see the work of his hands and stand amazed. They see God's power and might and are speechless.

I am no different. There is so much in nature and the heavens that declare the glory of God. I have also, however, been privileged to witness the power and glory of God within smaller spaces. I've seen him manifested in the Grand Canyon and I've also seen him manifested in my office. I have seen the power and glory of God through the mighty works of nature and through the miracle of changed lives. Both proclaim the work of his hands.

It is time for you to fully realize that you are also a "work of his hands." He formed your body (Psalm 139) and transforms your mind (Rom. 12:2). You are "fearfully and wonderfully made" (Ps. 139:14). You are a living, breathing, walking testimony to God. Do you feel that way? Do you look at yourself and see yourself as miraculous and marvelous as any work of nature? Do you feel within yourself the handprint of God? Do you see yourself as his active creation?

I suspect many of you would say no to those questions. You look out and believe in God's power to create mighty works in nature and in the heavens but consider yourself too hard a nut to crack. He is all-powerful when it comes to oceans and winds and storms but, somehow, his power stops at the doorway to your heart. He can create all that, yes, but change you? No.

Deep down, for many of you, there is still a voice that argues such a transformation from your old self of anger to a new self without that anger isn't possible. You believe God has the ability to change other people but don't believe he can pull off something like that for you. For others, it's possible; for you, it's impossible. Well, you know yourself pretty well. If you say it's an impossible task, then I am inclined to believe you. There's just one thing, as the verse above says—with God, everything is possible, including the impossible. With God, all things are possible—all things, including a radical change in how you live your life, how you view yourself, and how you interact with others.

God knows this to be true; now you must believe also. You must believe you are a work of his hands and that God is able to change you. You must be able to say along with Psalm 138:8: "The LORD will fulfill his purpose for me; your love, O LORD, endures forever—do not abandon the works of your hands." The prophet Isaiah puts it this way: "We are the clay, you are the potter; we are all the work of your hand" (Isa. 64:8). Your potter is able to do the impossible with you.

Accomplishing the Impossible

Do you remember Janice at the beginning of this book? She was the woman who was overwhelmed by her job, who endeavored never to show her anger and irritation at work but then seethed in the car on the way home and arrived tense and irritable. Or what about the young mother, Amy, who was still so angry and wounded over her divorce and her ex-husband that the whole world couldn't seem to contain the rage that kept sloshing onto her kids? Or midlife Marilyn, who seemingly had everything together but ended up finding fault with just about everything, alienating her from her husband and friends just when she finally had more time to give them?

For each of these women, their anger was intense, entrenched, and constant. Janice thought it was impossible to change because she never felt she had enough control over her life to do anything about the craziness. Amy doubted she could ever get over being mad at her ex-husband because he kept doing things that sent her over the edge. Marilyn didn't think she had an issue, so she saw no reason to change. For each, change did not seem possible.

Left to their own devices, they were right; change was not possible. They could not change because they did not believe they could or understand they needed to. Because their hearts were open to anger but not to change, they were stuck in their anger. Again, what was impossible for Janice, Amy, and Marilyn is eminently possible for God.

With God's help, Janice can learn that she doesn't need to say yes to everything in order to be considered valuable and accepted. She can learn to find her worth and approval from other sources than just her work. She can look to God as her loving Father. She can look to the family and friends she's been blessed with. With God's help, Janice can understand the meaning of a good day's work and the satisfaction of doing her best, even if that means she didn't get everything done. No longer under such intense self-pressure and stress at work, Janice can begin to view her co-workers as people instead of problems. She can begin to see her family as sources of comfort and delight instead of endless demands and distractions.

With God's help, Amy can learn to navigate how to be a mom and single. She can do so without the encumbering baggage of anger at her ex-husband. Amy can learn how to begin the process of forgiving him and forgiving herself for the end of their relationship. She can learn how to interact positively through the conduit of something they both agree on—the love of their children. Freed from her anger at their father, with God's help, Amy can spare her children further damage from the anger that so dominated their relationship. She can be free to heal and mend herself, in order to better help and assist her children in doing the same.

With God's help, Marilyn can open her eyes to how anger has affected her life. She can put aside the denial and learn to recognize the destructive patterns she's allowed to take root. With God's help, Marilyn can put down her need for perfectionism and pick up mercy and grace. She can finally stop looking to herself and her own actions for safety and security and look instead to God. With God's help, Marilyn can find rest and peace. When she does, so can all those around her.

Over the course of my life and professional career, I've met and worked with women like Janice, Amy, and Marilyn, as well as others you've read about in these chapters. All of them are different, with different backgrounds, different hurts, different stories, but each one is able to come to the same destination: a life controlled by love instead of a life overshadowed by anger.

Each one came to a point of decision. It's something you need to decide for yourself—will you continue to live a life submitted to your anger or will you choose a life submitted to God? You cannot hold on to the one and still choose the other. They are not compatible. You must give up the one in order to truly grasp on to the other. It's not unlike what Jesus talked about in Matthew 6:24. This verse is talking about money, but I think women can be just as controlled by their anger as people are by their money. What if you read the verse this way: "No one can serve two masters. Either she will hate the one and love the other, or she will be devoted to the one and despise the other. You cannot serve both God and *your anger.*"

Serving your anger has brought you pain, resentment, bitterness, and sorrow. God promises to give you love, joy, peace, patience, kindness, goodness, faithfulness, gentleness, and self-control. God is the better master.

If your anger springs from an injustice, an evil, a wrong against you, God will repay.

If your anger springs from unrealistic expectations and wishful thinking, God will renew your mind to see, understand, and appreciate the truth.

If your anger springs from guilt, shame, and fear, God will heal those wounds and replace them with peace, acceptance, and courage.

If your anger is so deeply engrained you can hardly tell where it comes from anymore, God will gently work the truth up to the surface so you can deal with it and move beyond.

If your anger is all you feel you have left in this world, God will open up your eyes to his endless promises and possibilities for your life.

All you need to do to start down this path is to *believe*.

All you need to do to continue down this path is to *act* on your belief.

With you, change is not certain; with God, it is. Remember, when you submit yourself to God, you take yourself out of the driver's seat of your life and turn it over to God. When God is in control, all things are possible, "for it is God who works in you to will and to act according to his good purpose" (Phil. 2:13).

There is no Note to Self section at the end of this chapter because your assignment is to simply go out and do what you've learned. Put it into practice.

- Start small.
- Be intentional.
- Be alert to yourself.
- Really listen to what you say to yourself and to others.
- When you need to be angry, use God as your punching bag.

- When you find yourself angry over the things God is angry about, pray and give it over to him since he's got it anyway.
- Actively invite and nurture positive thoughts and feelings.
- Practice an attitude of gratitude about life and other people.
- Don't sweat the small stuff.
- Forgive the big stuff.
- Leave room for God's wrath.
- Actively and intentionally replace love for anger.

Living a Life of Love

When you submit your life to God, you're really submitting your life to love, for 1 John 4:16 very plainly says that God is love. Will you still be angry at times? Yes, you will, because anger is part of your emotional repertoire, given to you by God. However, when you live a life of love, anger—when it comes—is placed into context. Anger, when it comes, doesn't get the stage all to itself; it must share the stage with other responses such as mercy, forgiveness, kindness, and gentleness. Mixed in with that kind of crowd, anger loses some of its volume and smoothes out some of its rougher edges.

Love is a counterbalance to anger. Here again are the attributes of love from 1 Corinthians 13:4–8:

Love is patient, love is kind. It does not envy, it does not boast, it is not proud. It is not rude, it is not self-seeking, it is not easily angered, it keeps no record of wrongs. Love does not delight in evil but rejoices with the truth. It always protects, always trusts, always hopes, always perseveres. Love never fails.

So, that is your assignment. Go out and practice living a life of love, filled with God's Spirit and the optimism, hope, and joy he brings. It's a big assignment, but your Mentor is as large as the universe itself. He's had a lot of practice, even practice where you are concerned, so he's able to help you.

More than anything else, open your heart and mind to God and his transforming power. Be patient but purposeful in your pursuit of love. Be patient with others; be patient with yourself. Wait upon the Lord, and he will renew your strength.

Notes

1. *Pacific Northwest*, July 28, 2002, http://community.seattle times. nwsource.com/archive/?date=20020728&slug=pdanger28.

2. http://www.sciencedaily.com/releases/2008/03/080310131529 .htm.

3. The International Journal of Psychophysiology Epub 2008 Jan 17 (http://www.ncbi.nlm.nih.gov/pubmed/18262673?ordinalpos=1& itool=EntrezSystem2.PEntrez.Pubmed.Pubmed_ResultsPanel.Pub med_ DiscoveryPanel.Pubmed_Discovery_RA&linkpos=3&log$=relatedarticl es&logdbfrom=pubmed).

4. Nancy Lee DeMoss, *Choosing Forgiveness* (Chicago: Moody, 2006), 99.

Gregory L. Jantz, PhD, is a popular speaker and award-winning author. He is a licensed mental health counselor and a certified chemical dependency professional. Dr. Jantz is the founder of The Center for Counseling and Health Resources, Inc., a leading mental health and chemical dependency healthcare facility, known as "a place of hope."

The Center for Counseling and Health Resources, Inc., is a whole-person treatment center. Individuals from across the United States as well as the rest of the world come to participate in the hope-filled work of recovery from a range of traumas and addictive behaviors. Dr. Jantz's whole-person approach addresses the emotional, relational, intellectual, physical, and spiritual dimensions of each person with a unique, tailored treatment plan.

His compassionate, solution-oriented viewpoints on timely topics, plus a natural gift for storytelling, make him a sought-after guest on local and national radio and television. He speaks nationally at conferences, seminars, and retreats on a wide variety of topics, utilizing his extensive expertise and experience.

Dr. Jantz has been married for twenty-five years to his wife, LaFon. They have two sons, Gregg and Benjamin.

Ann McMurray is a freelance writer living in Brier, Washington, whose partnership with Dr. Jantz goes back many years.

For more information about the work of The Center, please call The Center's toll-free number of 888-771-5166. You can also contact The Center through their website at www.aplaceofhope .com or by mail at P.O. Box 700, Edmonds, WA 98020.

Other Resources by Dr. Gregory Jantz

God Can Help You Heal

Happy for the Rest of Your Life

Healing the Scars of Emotional Abuse

Healthy Habits, Happy Kids: A Practical Plan to Help Your Family

Hope, Help and Healing for Eating Disorders

Moving Beyond Depression: A Whole-Person Approach to Healing

The Body God Designed: How to Love the Body You've Got While You Get the Body You Want

The Molding of a Champion: Helping Your Child Shape a Winning Destiny

The Total Temple Makeover: How to Turn Your Body into a Temple You Can Rejoice In

Thin Over 40: The Simple 12-Week Plan

Too Close to the Flame: Recognizing and Avoiding Sexualized Relationships

Turning the Tables on Gambling: Hope and Help for an Addictive Behavior

HOPE AND HEALING FOR THE VICTIMS OF EMOTIONAL ABUSE

GREGORY L. JANTZ, PhD
WITH ANN McMURRAY

Healing the Scars of Emotional Abuse

REVISED AND UPDATED

Revell
a division of Baker Publishing Group
www.RevellBooks.com

YOU CAN LIVE FREE FROM ANXIETY

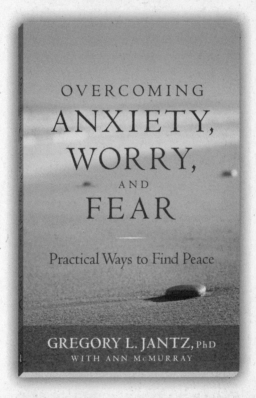

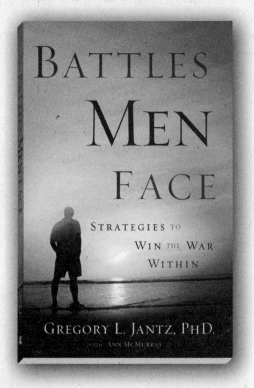